# 99+ EASY HOME CANNING RECIPES

How to Preserve Your Harvest, Live Greener, Eat Healthier, Feed Your Family & Prepare for Hard Times

---

BY
LUKE POTTER

## THE URBAN FARMER

Luke Potter

Copyright © 2023 Luke Potter All rights reserved.

The content contained within this book may not be reproduced, duplicated, or transmitted without direct written permission from the author or the publisher.

Under no circumstances will any blame or legal responsibility be held against the publisher, or author, for any damages, reparation, or monetary loss due to the information contained within this book. Either directly or indirectly. You are responsible for your own choices, actions, and results.

**Legal Notice:**

This book is copyright protected. This book is only for personal use. You cannot amend, distribute, sell, use, quote, or paraphrase any part, or the content within this book, without the consent of the author or publisher.

**Disclaimer Notice:**

Please note the information contained within this document is for educational and entertainment purposes only. All effort has been executed to present accurate, up-to-date, and reliable, complete information. No warranties of any kind are declared or implied. Readers acknowledge that the author is not engaging in the rendering of legal, financial, medical, or professional advice. The content within this book has been derived from various sources. Please consult a licensed professional before attempting any techniques outlined in this book.

By reading this document, the reader agrees that under no circumstances is the author responsible for any losses, direct or indirect, which are incurred as a result of the use of the information contained within this document, including, but not limited to, errors, omissions, or inaccuracies.

# DEDICATION

This book is dedicated to the generations of homemakers, especially my grandmother and mom, who grew Victory Gardens during WWII to help the war effort while feeding their families healthy, nutritious food.

And to the home canners who kept their families alive during The Great Depression and The Dust Bowl.

And to the modern-day homesteaders and preppers who prefer a simpler, more sustainable lifestyle.

And to the millions of people around the world who took up gardening and home canning during the recent pandemic.

We take this vow:
*"Our families, loved ones, and neighbors will never go hungry because we prepared for the worst of times while praying for the best of times".*

My Ancestral Family Homestead in Maine

*Proverbs 21:20*
*"The wise store up choice food and olive oil, while fools gulp theirs down."*

# Contents

INTRODUCTION to 99+ EASY HOME CANNING RECIPES . . . . . . . .9
THE BASICS . . . . . . . . . . . . . . . . . . . . . . . . . . . . . . . . . . . . . . . . . . . . .20
CANNING METHODS . . . . . . . . . . . . . . . . . . . . . . . . . . . . . . . . . . .23
Processing Times Guide . . . . . . . . . . . . . . . . . . . . . . . . . . . . . . . .27
GLOSSARY & ABBREVIATIONS. . . . . . . . . . . . . . . . . . . . . . . . . . .28

**SOUPS & STEWS** . . . . . . . . . . . . . . . . . . . . . . . . . . . . . . . . . . . . . **30**
    Comfort Food Chicken Soup . . . . . . . . . . . . . . . . . . . . . . . . . . .31
    Traditional Soup Stock . . . . . . . . . . . . . . . . . . . . . . . . . . . . . . . .32
    Vintage Clam Chowder . . . . . . . . . . . . . . . . . . . . . . . . . . . . . . . .33
    Homestyle Beef Stew with Vegetables . . . . . . . . . . . . . . . . . . . .34
    Homestead Prepper Split Pea Soup . . . . . . . . . . . . . . . . . . . . .36
    Classic Tomato Soup . . . . . . . . . . . . . . . . . . . . . . . . . . . . . . . . .37
    Italian Bread Soup . . . . . . . . . . . . . . . . . . . . . . . . . . . . . . . . . . .38
    Leek and Potato Soup . . . . . . . . . . . . . . . . . . . . . . . . . . . . . . . .40
    Meatless Spaghetti Sauce with Vegetables . . . . . . . . . . . . . . . .41
    Chili con Carne . . . . . . . . . . . . . . . . . . . . . . . . . . . . . . . . . . . . .42
    Meatless Chili . . . . . . . . . . . . . . . . . . . . . . . . . . . . . . . . . . . . . .43
    New England Boiled Dinner . . . . . . . . . . . . . . . . . . . . . . . . . . .44
    Vegetable Soup . . . . . . . . . . . . . . . . . . . . . . . . . . . . . . . . . . . . .45

**JUICES** . . . . . . . . . . . . . . . . . . . . . . . . . . . . . . . . . . . . . . . . . . . . . **46**
    Cranberry Juice . . . . . . . . . . . . . . . . . . . . . . . . . . . . . . . . . . . . .47
    Spicy Vegetable Juice Cocktail . . . . . . . . . . . . . . . . . . . . . . . . .48
    Concord Grape Juice . . . . . . . . . . . . . . . . . . . . . . . . . . . . . . . . .49
    Pineapple Juice . . . . . . . . . . . . . . . . . . . . . . . . . . . . . . . . . . . . .50
    Grapefruit Juice . . . . . . . . . . . . . . . . . . . . . . . . . . . . . . . . . . . . .51
    Apple Juice . . . . . . . . . . . . . . . . . . . . . . . . . . . . . . . . . . . . . . . .52

## FRUITS ... 53
- Fruit Cocktail ... 54
- Whole Berry Cranberry Sauce ... 56
- Applesauce ... 57
- Perfect Peaches ... 59
- Blueberries ... 61
- Pears ... 62
- Old-Fashioned Red Cinnamon Apples ... 64

## PIE FILLINGS ... 66
- Easy as Apple Pie Filling ... 67
- Mom's Strawberry Rhubarb Pie Filling ... 69
- Blueberry Pie Filling ... 70
- Meatless Mincemeat Pie Filling ... 71
- Old-Fashioned Green Tomato Mincemeat Pie Filling ... 72
- Peach Pie Filling ... 73
- Pumpkin or Squash Pie Filling ... 74

## VEGETABLES ... 76
- Ma's Classic Green Beans ... 77
- Stewed Tomatoes and Vegetables ... 79
- Vintage Stewed Tomatoes and Vegetables ... 80
- Whole Kernel Corn ... 81
- Easy Creamed Corn ... 82
- Green Peas ... 83
- Winter Squash ... 84
- Carrots ... 85
- Greens ... 86
- Beets ... 87
- Okra ... 88
- Sweet Potatoes ... 89
- White, Red and Yellow Potatoes ... 90

## JELLIES, JAMS, FRUIT BUTTERS & MARMALADES ....... 91

- Concord Grape Jelly ................................................. 92
- Granny's Apple Jelly .................................................. 94
- Rose Hip Jelly .......................................................... 96
- Fresh Blueberry Jelly ................................................ 98
- Strawberry Jelly ..................................................... 100
- Hot Sriracha Pepper Jelly ....................................... 101
- Fresh Herb Jelly ..................................................... 103
- Lemon and Lavender Jelly .................................... 104
- Patten's Farm Stand Strawberry Jam ..................... 105
- Blueberry Jam ....................................................... 106
- Triple Berry Jam .................................................... 107
- Raspberry Jam ...................................................... 108
- Queen's Jam .......................................................... 109
- New England Apple Cider Butter ........................... 110
- Traditional Orange Marmalade .............................. 112
- Old-Fashioned Carrot and Orange Marmalade ...... 114
- Strawberry Lemon Marmalade .............................. 116

## PICKLES & PICKLED VEGETABLES ................... 117

- Grammie's Victory Garden Dill Pickles .................. 118
- Old-Fashioned Cucumber and Onion Pickles ........ 120
- Bread and Butter Pickles ....................................... 122
- Watermelon Rind Pickles ...................................... 123
- Down East Sour Pickles ........................................ 125
- Ice Water Pickle Spears ........................................ 126
- End of Harvest Pickled Vegetable Mix .................. 127
- Pickled Red Cabbage ............................................ 128
- Dilly Beans ............................................................ 129
- Dilly Carrots .......................................................... 131
- Do Chua (Vietnamese Carrot and Daikon Radish Pickles) ...... 132
- Sweet Pickled Beets .............................................. 134

Traditional Fermented Sauerkraut . . . . . . . . . . . . . . . . . . . . . . . . . . . 136
State Fair Pickled Three-Bean Salad . . . . . . . . . . . . . . . . . . . . . . . . . 137
No-Cook Pickled Hot Pepper Mix . . . . . . . . . . . . . . . . . . . . . . . . . . . 139
Pickled Hot Peppers . . . . . . . . . . . . . . . . . . . . . . . . . . . . . . . . . . . . . 141
14-Day Sweet Pickles. . . . . . . . . . . . . . . . . . . . . . . . . . . . . . . . . . . . . 142

**RELISHES & SALSA** . . . . . . . . . . . . . . . . . . . . . . . . . . . . . . . . . . . . . . **144**
Taste of Summer Vegetable Salsa. . . . . . . . . . . . . . . . . . . . . . . . . . . . 145
Sweet Relish . . . . . . . . . . . . . . . . . . . . . . . . . . . . . . . . . . . . . . . . . . . . 147
Dill Relish . . . . . . . . . . . . . . . . . . . . . . . . . . . . . . . . . . . . . . . . . . . . . . 148
Victory Garden Red Pepper Relish . . . . . . . . . . . . . . . . . . . . . . . . . . 149
County Fair Corn Relish. . . . . . . . . . . . . . . . . . . . . . . . . . . . . . . . . . . 150
Green Tomato Relish. . . . . . . . . . . . . . . . . . . . . . . . . . . . . . . . . . . . . 151

**VINEGARS** . . . . . . . . . . . . . . . . . . . . . . . . . . . . . . . . . . . . . . . . . . . . . . **152**
Legendary 4 Thieves Vinegar Tonic . . . . . . . . . . . . . . . . . . . . . . . . . 153
Raspberry Vinegar. . . . . . . . . . . . . . . . . . . . . . . . . . . . . . . . . . . . . . . 155
Tarragon Vinegar. . . . . . . . . . . . . . . . . . . . . . . . . . . . . . . . . . . . . . . . 156
Blueberry and Basil Vinegar. . . . . . . . . . . . . . . . . . . . . . . . . . . . . . . 157

**MEAT, POULTRY & FISH** . . . . . . . . . . . . . . . . . . . . . . . . . . . . . . . . . **158**
Canned Chicken . . . . . . . . . . . . . . . . . . . . . . . . . . . . . . . . . . . . . . . . 159
Italian Meatballs in Sauce. . . . . . . . . . . . . . . . . . . . . . . . . . . . . . . . . 161
Chicken a la King. . . . . . . . . . . . . . . . . . . . . . . . . . . . . . . . . . . . . . . 162
Ground Meat . . . . . . . . . . . . . . . . . . . . . . . . . . . . . . . . . . . . . . . . . . 164
Venison and Game. . . . . . . . . . . . . . . . . . . . . . . . . . . . . . . . . . . . . . 166
Fish. . . . . . . . . . . . . . . . . . . . . . . . . . . . . . . . . . . . . . . . . . . . . . . . . . . 168

OTHER PRESERVATION METHODS . . . . . . . . . . . . . . . . . . . . . . . . 169
TROUBLESHOOTING. . . . . . . . . . . . . . . . . . . . . . . . . . . . . . . . . . . . . 173
CONCLUSION. . . . . . . . . . . . . . . . . . . . . . . . . . . . . . . . . . . . . . . . . . . 176
ABOUT THE AUTHOR. . . . . . . . . . . . . . . . . . . . . . . . . . . . . . . . . . . . 179
RESOURCES. . . . . . . . . . . . . . . . . . . . . . . . . . . . . . . . . . . . . . . . . . . . 180
INDEX OF RECIPES. . . . . . . . . . . . . . . . . . . . . . . . . . . . . . . . . . . . . . 182
My Canning Journal. . . . . . . . . . . . . . . . . . . . . . . . . . . . . . . . . . . . . . 184

Other books by Luke Potter
Available worldwide on Amazon

# INTRODUCTION to 99+ EASY HOME CANNING RECIPES

## My Story

I've dedicated my adult life to gardening and preserving my harvest. I learned these life skills from my Canadian-born grandmother, who raised two daughters on her own during The Great Depression and WWII. For her, gardening and home canning was not a hobby. It meant food and survival for her family. My mom continued the family traditions, and I learned in the kitchen at her feet. My first job was on a farm. It was demanding work and little pay, but I learned how things grow and what to do with the harvest to make it last all year. To this day, nothing makes me happier than when I'm growing and canning my own food.

Many of these home canning recipes were handed down from generation to generation on hand-written recipe cards. So that you know, they all meet or exceed modern-day food safety standards. These are tried-and-true recipes that are simple to follow even if you've never canned before. I teach many of these same recipes to children in my homeschool canning classes. If they can do it, so can you!

I've tried and evaluated many different recipes during many decades of home canning, but these easy recipes simply produce the most delicious, jaw-dropping results! Nothing beats the genuine flavor of home-grown green beans or tomatoes in the dead of winter. Plus, you'll have an emergency backup supply of nutritious food for your family if, for some reason, you can't get to the grocery store or there are food shortages – either natural, fabricated or disaster-related

So, let's roll up our sleeves, get our aprons on and dive right in. I guarantee you'll enjoy the satisfying Zen-like process of home canning and take tremendous pride in the results!

## Introduction to Canning Food

Home canning, also known colloquially as "putting up food" or processing, is the method of preserving foods, especially fruits, vegetables, and meats, by packing them into glass jars and then heating the jars to create a vacuum seal and killing the organisms that would otherwise cause spoilage.

Two methods are used in home canning. One is the hot water bath for foods high in acid or sugars like tomatoes and jams. The other requires a pressure canner for low acid foods like meats, stews, carrots, and green beans. Food properly processed and stored in canning jars has a stable shelf life of 18 months or longer without refrigeration.

Mason jars were developed in 1858 by John Mason. Soon other companies began manufacturing canning jars, but they are all commonly referred to as Mason jars regardless of the manufacturer. They are available in a variety of sizes in either wide-mouth or regular mouth styles.

For the hot water bath method, you simply need a large pot with a lid, deep enough, so your jars will be covered with an inch or two of boiling water. You'll also need a rack to keep your jars off the bottom of the pot to prevent breakage. For pressure canning, you'll need a pressure canner. They are available in various sizes. The capacity will determine the number of jars it will hold. When manufacturer directions are followed, they are entirely safe to use.

**History of Home Canning**

It used to be that homemakers canned fresh fruits and vegetables for consumption during the winter months before modern farming techniques and global transportation made fresh produce available year-round. Nowadays, many people practice home canning for the same reasons because it extends and preserves the harvest. Plus, if you have an abundant garden, and you should after reading my book How to Grow Vegetables in Pots & Containers, there are only so many tomatoes, beans, and cucumbers you can eat when faced with a harvest of bushels of fresh produce. And it simply makes meal prep easier. You have a ready stockpile of prepared food on hand. If you want a bowl of tomato soup, just reheat a pint. You did all the prep work months before. Want some pickles? Just open the pantry or cupboard. Can't make it to the market because of a blizzard, hurricane, or disaster? Your family won't go hungry because you prepared in advance. When I can at home, I'm reminded of the fable of the ant and the grasshopper. The ant prepared for the winter while the grasshopper played and fiddled the summer away. When winter came, and he had no food to eat, the ant turned him away, and the grasshopper starved. The moral being, be prepared. There's a time for work, and there's a time for play. I always joke with my neighbors that they know which house has food stored up when the zombie apocalypse comes!

Like millions of others, perhaps you took up home gardening and canning during the recent pandemic - just like our ancestors had done during earlier times of national struggle and food shortages. Let's take a brief historical look at the history of home canning before diving into the recipes.

## Napoleonic Wars – Malnutrition

Since before written history, humans have preserved food by drying, smoking, salting, and fermenting. Home canning in glass jars is a relatively recent development in the long history of food preservation.

Napoleon said, "An army travels on its stomach." Meaning that without a consistent supply of food, either when his naval forces were at sea or his troops were thousands of miles from home marching towards Russia, they were destined to fail. It is believed, more of Napoleon's troops died of malnutrition and disease during his ill-fated Russian campaign than perished from battle.

Napoleon offered a prize to the person who could develop a method of safe food preservation for his constantly traveling military forces. The winner of the reward was Nicholas Appert. He developed a technique of heat-processing food in glass jars and bottles. Some claim that the first "bottling" was invented by Napoleon's troops, who would ladle hot soup into empty wine bottles and carry them into battle or on to the next encampment. The troops sealed these bottles with corks, wire, and paraffin.

## US Civil War – A Nation Divided

During the US Civil War, glass jars with glass lids, rubber rings, and a wire and bale locking mechanism were developed, making it easier for homemakers, and the war machine, to preserve the harvest while supplying the troops on both sides of the battle. These locking jars became the standard for home canning for nearly 100 years.

## WWI – War Gardens

In 1915, Alexander Kerr invented the modern-day two-piece metal lid and screw band to seal glass canning jars. This is the sealing method that we still utilize today. Also, during WWI, the first "War Gardens" began in the United States, United Kingdom, Canada, Australia, and Germany. In these nations at war, citizens, including school children, were encouraged, through public campaigns, to plant vegetable gardens to supplement their rations, allowing more food to be diverted to the troops. Gardening was also encouraged to boost morale. Citizens planted gardens in both public parks and private residences. Just like the recent pandemic, many people grew gardens for the first time. It is estimated that over five million War Gardens were planted in the United States alone.

Faced with abundant harvests, homemakers learned to can what they could not consume, give away, or preserve by other means. Coupled with the technological advances introduced by the Ball and Kerr companies, home canning enjoyed its first boom.

## The Great Depression – Hard Times

Following a period of economic vitality, The Great Depression and The Dust Bowl devasted America in the 1930s. Grain became scarce as the topsoil blew away in the Great Plains. Without feed, livestock was slaughtered or died. Another disaster created another surge in home canning, and it was simply cheaper to grow and can your own food. Homemakers in the Dust Bowl states resorted to pickling and canning nettles to keep their families alive. Hard times required folks to become more self-reliant to survive.

## WWII – Victory Gardens

Another World War – this one was more extensive in scale. War Gardens were renamed Victory Gardens to boost morale and lower the military's cost of food. At the height of the War in 1943, there were 18 million Victory Gardens in the United States – 12 million in cities and 6 million on farms. Even First Lady Eleanor Roosevelt had a Victory Garden planted at the White House. During the War, gardening was considered a patriotic duty.

*"A Victory Garden is like a share in an airplane factory. It helps win the War and it pays dividends too."* Claude Wickard, U.S. Secretary of Agriculture

And with all those gardens, and the mass production of glass canning jars by Ball, Atlas, Kerr, and others, home canning surged to new heights. In 1943, home canning peaked with more than 4 billion jars processed. The sheer amount of home-grown food was awe-inspiring. By 1944, home production of fruits and vegetables equaled what was commercially grown. After the War, home gardening declined as the population moved to the suburbs, and kitchen gardens were replaced with the well-manicured lawns of the 1950s and 1960s. Home canning also declined with the mass marketing of home freezers. Of course, some people continued to garden and practice home canning to preserve their harvest.

## 1970s – Back to Basics

With gas shortages, double-digit inflation, and the back-to-basics movement, home canning regained popularity in the 1970s.

## Pandemic – Self-reliance

In 2020, a worldwide pandemic appeared out of nowhere. And the lockdowns coincided with the start of the gardening season. Stores and nurseries were ordered closed. Walmart cordoned off their gardening section as "non-essential." Seeds became unavailable, except through mail order companies, which quickly sold out. It is estimated that home gardening increased by 300% during the coronavirus pandemic. People were isolated in their homes, unable to work, and had time on their hands. Plus, everyday items were simply unavailable. Meat, eggs, and everyday food items were rationed. With the fear of food shortages, people took up home gardening. Once again, a crisis compelled people back to nature. Spending time in the sun, working in the dirt, and tending our gardens was therapeutic and nurturing when the world seemed to be falling apart.

Vitamin D boosted our immune systems. Sunlight relieved depression. And the pandemic gardeners learned to can their harvest so their pantries would be well-stocked. Their families would not go hungry. Many of these first-time gardeners and canners vowed to become life-long gardeners and home canners. They realized how quickly things can go awry and that it pays to be prepared.

**Preppers – Survival**

In the 21st century, a new movement began to take hold. Harkening back to the Cold War Era, people, fearing the uncertainty of the future, witnessing social and political unrest, and the erosion of civil liberties, began preparing for when SHTF and society as we know it collapses. Survivalists, or preppers, began living off-grid, homesteading, building bomb shelters, gathering weapons, practicing low-tech life skills, and stockpiling food. These forward-thinking individualists raise chickens, livestock and grow and preserve their food. There are food preservation books specifically marketed to preppers and survivalists.

**Conclusion**

*"In times of great stress or adversity, it's always best to keep busy, to plow your anger and your energy into something positive."* Lee Iacocca

I'm convinced there is something inherent in our human DNA instructing us to grow and preserve food in times of great stress and adversity. It's our ancient primal survival instinct at work. And because of that, there will always be home gardeners. There will always be home canners. The cities may collapse. The grid may go down. There may be war. But we will grow food. And our families will not go hungry because we have learned how to preserve our abundant harvests. Join me on this self-reliant, sustainable journey. You'll never look back.

PLANT A GARDEN
for VICTORY
POST MAY 1 ST. TO 15 TH.
WAR PRODUCTION CO-ORDINATING COMMITTEE

# PLANT A VICTORY GARDEN

**OUR FOOD IS FIGHTING**

A GARDEN WILL MAKE YOUR RATIONS GO FURTHER

# THE BASICS

## The Science

Let's begin with a science lesson. Food spoils because of the presence of molds, yeast, and bacteria. They exist in nature and are on the food, in water, air, and soil - even in the canning jars we use. Canning stops their action by the application of heat and the removal of air from the jars. The heat kills molds, yeast, and bacteria in the food and jars. The vacuum-sealed lid is airtight and prevents micro-organisms from entering the jar after canning. This makes canned goods shelf-stable without refrigeration for 18 months or longer.

Boiling water stops the action of yeasts and molds. Short exposure to boiling water will neutralize the enzymes found in all vegetables, fruits, and meats. Unless the actions of enzymes are stopped, they can bring about unwanted changes such as discoloration, softened texture, loss of flavor, and destruction of Vitamin C.

Bacteria are more challenging to destroy. There are several types of bacteria, some of which are more heat resistant. Like tomatoes and many fruits, acidic foods help prevent the growth of bacteria and are the easiest to can. If not destroyed by heat during the canning process, yeast and many bacteria can grow in a sealed jar. A sure sign that bacteria or yeast is present is the seal has popped, the lid is not secure, and there is an odor or discoloration. This means you did not use sufficient heat during the canning process, and the food has spoiled. If you notice any of these indicators, dispose of the food at once, and sterilize the jar. DO NOT taste test suspicious canned food to see if it has spoiled. You'll risk botulism. With home canning, it's better safe than sorry. To avoid problems like spoilage, always process food the full time suggested in the recipes, adjusting for your altitude. Use the hot water bath method or pressure canner method as shown in the recipe.

**Start Fresh**

You can't make a silk purse out of a sow's ear, so start by selecting vegetables, fruits, and meats in excellent condition. Fruits and vegetables that are overripe may not process correctly. Produce with blemishes, soft spots, or rotten spots may spoil your entire product, so make sure to cut these out and discard them. Process meats as soon as possible to avoid spoilage. The quality of fruits and vegetables deteriorates quickly, so I like to harvest and be ready to can immediately. Prepare your canner and jars and gather all your supplies in advance of harvesting, and you'll capture the maximum garden-fresh flavor and nutrition.

And make sure to read the recipe thoroughly before beginning so you'll know what to have on hand, how to proceed, the method to use, and the time required from start to finish. When you plan ahead, you'll find home canning is easy, fun, and therapeutic. You'll experience a Zen-like delight as you see your pantry fill up with jars of healthy, nutritious food. You'll feel a well-earned sense of pride in your accomplishment.

# CANNING METHODS

Canning is one of the best ways to preserve food easily and quickly. It's also a low-tech operation that requires only a few standard kitchen instruments to be successful. The most important thing about canning is to make sure you select high-quality canning jars that have seals and lids in good condition. Ensure the jars have no chips or cracks, as these can cause breakage during the canning process. At a minimum, clean your jars thoroughly with dish soap and hot water before use. Or use a food-grade sanitizer. I run mine through the dishwasher cycle using hot water before canning to ensure no fungi or bacteria contaminate the contents.

**Steps for Hot Water Bath Canning**

Hot water bath canning is a suitable method for preserving high-acid foods. This includes most fruits and pickled vegetables. Low-acid foods run the risk of developing the bacterial spore that causes botulism. You'll need to add citric acid to safely can or use a pressure canner for canning low-acid vegetables and all meats.

The first step is to heat your clean, sterile jars in a large pot of hot water deep enough to cover the jars fully. Fill the jars and kettle with water and put them on low heat. Place the lids and bands in water in a saucepan over low heat until you are ready to use them. Remember, you can only use lids once. You can reuse the bands and jars indefinitely.

## Preparing Fruit and Vegetables for Canning

There are two ways to preserve your harvest using the hot water bath: raw and heated. The raw pack method is self-explanatory. You'll simply chop the fruit or vegetable up enough to fit in the jar and fill the rest with boiling water or syrup. Heating the fruits and vegetables to boiling before putting them in the jars yields a better flavor and color. You can use the liquid from heating to fill the canning jar. The heating process reduces the risk of your preserves shrinking and leaving too much space at the top of the jar.

A canning rack keeps the bottom of the jars from touching the pot, which can cause excessive heat and may break your jars. If you don't have a canning rack, you can use a pressure canner insert, a cake cooling rack, or even a folded kitchen towel to prevent the jars from breaking.

You'll want to find a recipe specifically for the type of fruits and vegetables you're canning. There will be a recommended headspace in the jar that prevents over or under-filling. Using a jar lifter, remove one jar at a time from the hot water kettle and drain the water back into the pot. Immediately fill the jar, making sure to use a rubber spatula to scrape around the inside of the jar to free trapped air bubbles.

Wipe the rims, place the lids and pressure bands on the jars, and tighten until just finger tight. You don't want to overtighten the bands because the jars can explode. Air needs to escape during the canning process. Set the jar on the canning rack before getting the next jar from the hot water. Don't let the jars touch on the canning rack.

If you are canning raw fruit and vegetables, start with the water hot but not boiling. Fruits and vegetables heated first should go into softly boiling water. Add enough boiling water to ensure at least one inch of depth above the jars.

Raise the temperature to a steady, rolling boil, then cover and set a timer according to your recipe. When the processing is finished, turn off the heat, remove the lid, wait 5 minutes, and gently remove each jar from the water. Place them on an elevated rack or dry cloth at least one inch apart. This will prevent sudden temperature changes that can result in jar breakage or even dangerous explosions. Do not touch the pressure rings or metal lids. Let the cans cool on their own before handling. Don't forget to label and date them.

## Pressure Canner Method

The pressure canner method of canning is the only safe way to can low-acid foods like most vegetables. This is also how you preserve meat, poultry, and seafood. You'll prepare for canning in a pressure canner just the same as for canning in the hot water bath, and the difference is that you'll put only two or three inches of water in the pressure canner rather than submerging the jars.

Once the pressure canner is filled with jars ready for canning, lock the lid in place. Turn the heat on high and let the temperature rise quickly. This will rapidly increase the pressure in the cooker. When steam begins to hiss from the vent pipe, set your timer for 5-10 minutes, then place the gauge in place. Most recipes call for 10 pounds pressure. Lower the burner slightly until the gauge "jiggles" 3-4 times per minute. This lets the pressure build gradually, making it easier to settle the pressure at the proper temperature. There are modern pressure canners that don't work with a weighted gauge. Follow the manufacturer's directions for the pressure canner you are using.

Follow the guidelines in your recipe for the length of time to process your harvest in a pressure canner. Most fruit and vegetable recipes will require 20-45 minutes per pint - longer for quarts. When the time is up, turn off the heat and move the pressure canner off the burner if possible. Do not remove the vent cap or try to open the lid. Pressure will gradually decrease. You'll leave the cooker alone for 30-45 minutes or longer, depending on the style, size, and thickness of your cooker.

Once you remove the lid, gently lift the jars from the canner using a jar lifter. Arrange them on a cooling rack, or dry dish towel, at least one inch apart, and let them cool. You'll hear a "ping" as the jars cool, showing you have a successful seal. After the jars are thoroughly cooled, check the seal by gently pressing on the metal lid, and it should not pop up or down. Refrigerate any cans that didn't seal properly. You can remove the bands and label your jars. It's a good idea to write down the date you canned the contents. That way, you are practicing proper food rotation when consuming your harvest.

Each of the recipes in this book specifies the canning method, processing time, and specific instructions.

# Processing Times Guide

For successful and safe home-canning, using either method, you need to adjust processing times based on the altitude of your location. Use this chart:

Times listed are for 0 to 1,000 feet above sea level

Increase by 5 minutes for 1,001 feet to 3,000 feet

Increase by 10 minutes for 3,001 feet to 6,000 feet

Increase by 15 minutes for 6,001 feet to 8,000 feet

Increase by 20 minutes for 8,001 feet to 10,000 feet

You can check your elevation at: https://whatismyelevation.com

# GLOSSARY & ABBREVIATIONS

**Altitude** = The height of your residence in relation to sea level.
**Alum** = A colorless astringent compound available online or in the spice section.
**Bands** = The metal rings used to secure lids on canning jars.
**Blanching** = Brief immersion of food in boiling water.
**Brine** = Salted water used in food preservation.
**Cup** = 8 ounces or 237 ml
**ClearJel** = A food starch used for thickening in canning.
**Cold-pack/Raw-pack** = When raw, uncooked food is added to canning jars.
**Finger tight** = Hand tightening without the use of a tool.
**Hard boil/Rolling boil** = A boiling liquid that cannot be stirred down.
**Headspace** = Space in a canning jar between the food or liquid and the lid.
**High-acid** = A food or product with a pH of less than 4.6.
**Hot-pack** = When food is partially or fully cooked before adding to canning jars.
**Jelly** = A sweet spread of fruit juice, sugar, and sometimes pectin that is typically transparent.
**Canning salt** = Often sold as canning salt, kosher salt, or pickling salt. These are salts containing no iodine, which are used for canning.
**lb** = Pound or 16 ounces or 2.2 kg
**Lemon juice** = Use either freshly squeezed or bottled.
**Lids** = The metallic lids used for canning. Single use only. You cannot reuse them.
**Low-acid** = A food or product with a pH of more than 4.6.
**Marmalade** = A preserve made typically from citrus fruit.
**Mason jar** = Any airtight glass jar with a screw-top used for home canning.
**oz** = Ounces
**Pectin** = An extract from ripe fruits used as a setting agent in jams and jellies. Sold in either liquid or powdered form.
**Pickle Crisp** = Calcium chloride used as a firming agent in pickling.
**Pint** = 16 ounces or 473 ml
**PSI** = Pound-force per square inch

**Quart** = 32 ounces or .95 liter
**Relish** = A cooked and pickled product made of chopped vegetables, fruits, etc., used as a condiment.
**Simmer** = When food is cooked at a temperature just below boiling.
**Skimming** = The removal of impurities from the surface of a liquid while it is cooking.
**Soft boil** = When the surface of a liquid being heated is barely moving with occasional tiny bubbles rising to the surface.
**Sterilize** = To make something free from bacteria or other living organisms.
**tsp = Teaspoon or 5 ml**
**Tbsp** = Tablespoon or 15 ml

# SOUPS & STEWS

When you can a big batch of your favorite soup or stew, you'll always have a meal ready. Simply reheat and enjoy the garden-fresh flavors!

# Comfort Food Chicken Soup

The cure for what ails you!

## INGREDIENTS

- 16 cups chicken stock (store-bought or homemade)
- 3 cups diced cooked chicken
- 1½ cups peeled, sliced, or diced carrots
- 1½ cups chopped celery
- 1 cup finely chopped yellow or white onions
- Canning salt and freshly ground black pepper to taste
- 3 chicken or vegetable bouillon cubes (optional)

## YIELD

8 pints or 4 quarts

## Variations

Substitute 3 cups diced, cooked turkey in place of chicken. Add rice, orzo, or noodles when reheating.

## RECIPE

1. In a large stainless-steel saucepan, combine all ingredients. Bring to a boil over medium-high heat. Reduce heat and boil gently for 30 minutes. Add salt and pepper to taste. Add bouillon cubes if using.
2. Using a jar funnel, ladle hot soup into hot jars, leaving 1-inch headspace.
3. Wipe rims with a paper towel moistened with vinegar, add lids and bands. Hand-tighten.
4. Carefully place jars on rack in pressure canner. Attach and secure canner lid. Heat until canner starts hissing, then add gauge and begin timing after the first jiggle. Process pints for 75 minutes and quarts for 90 minutes at 10 pounds pressure. Adjust timing for higher altitudes.
5. Remove canner from heat. Allow pressure to decrease naturally.
6. Remove lid. Remove jars from the canner after 5 minutes. Cool on a wire rack or kitchen towel. Remove bands, label jars, and store them in a cool, dark place.

# Traditional Soup Stock

Prepare ahead and have it on hand when you're ready to make soup or homemade gravy.

## INGREDIENTS

- Bones, skin, trimmings of meat, poultry, or fish
- 1 onion chopped
- 1 celery stalk chopped
- 1 carrot chopped
- Water
- Canning salt

## YIELD

Varies

## RECIPE

1. Prepare pressure canner, jars, and lids.
2. Add bones, skin, and trimmings of meat, game, fish, or poultry to a large stainless-steel stockpot. Add one onion, 1 stalk of celery, and 1 carrot. Add water to cover and 1-2 tsp canning salt to taste. Bring to a boil, reduce heat and simmer for 1-2 hours. Add more boiling water if needed.
3. Using a colander, strain the liquid stock into a large bowl. Discard bones and vegetables. Meat pieces may be added to stock if desired.
4. Using a jar funnel, pour the stock into jars. Wipe rims, add lids and bands, and process pints for 45 minutes at 10 pounds pressure or 3 hours in a boiling hot water bath.

# Vintage Clam Chowder

A staple of Down East families. Add cream or milk when reheating to make New England-style clam chowder.

## INGREDIENTS

- 4 peeled, diced potatoes
- 1 lb fresh clams, rinsed, shelled, and chopped finely
- 2 large onions chopped fine
- 2 stalks celery chopped
- ½ tsp paprika
- 2 Tbsp butter
- Canning salt and freshly ground black pepper to taste

## YIELD

3-4 pints

## Luke's Variations

- Substitute 1 lb cut-up skinless fish for clams to make fish chowder.
- Add 1 or 2 large peeled, chopped tomatoes to make Manhattan-style clam chowder.

## RECIPE

1. In a large stainless-steel saucepan, mix all ingredients. Bring to a boil over medium-high heat. Reduce heat and boil gently for 15 minutes stirring often to prevent sticking.
2. Using a jar funnel, ladle hot chowder into hot jars, leaving 1-inch headspace.
3. Wipe rims with a paper towel moistened with vinegar. Add lids and bands. Hand-tighten.
4. Carefully place jars on rack in pressure canner. Attach and secure canner lid. Heat until canner starts hissing, then add gauge and begin timing after the first jiggle. Process pints for 90 minutes at 10 pounds pressure. Adjust timing for higher altitudes.
5. Remove canner from heat. Allow pressure to decrease naturally.
6. Remove lid. Remove jars from the canner after 5 minutes. Cool on a wire rack or kitchen towel. Remove bands, label jars, and store them in a cool, dark place.

# Homestyle Beef Stew with Vegetables

Dinty who? Serve this on a crisp, cold night with some crusty bread to sop up the gravy!

## INGREDIENTS

- 4-5 lbs stew beef cut into cubes
- 12 cups peeled, cubed potatoes
- 8 cups thickly sliced carrots
- 3 cups chopped celery
- 3 cups chopped onions
- 5 tsp canning salt
- 1 tsp dried thyme
- Freshly ground black pepper to taste
- Boiling water

## YIELD

14 pints or 7 quarts

## Luke's Variations

- Don't peel carrots for a more rustic style stew.
- Use petite carrots whole or cut in half depending on size.
- Substitute beef bone broth for boiling water.
- Use 3 cups whole peeled pearl onions instead of chopped onions.

## RECIPE

1. Prepare pressure canner, jars, and lids.
2. Heat oil over medium-high heat and brown beef cubes on all sides in a large skillet, adding more oil as needed. Drain oil after browning.
3. Add beef and all other ingredients to a large stainless-steel pot. Add boiling water to cover. Bring to a boil, occasionally stirring to prevent sticking. Reduce heat and simmer until stew begins to thicken.
4. Using a jar funnel, ladle hot stew into hot jars, leaving 1-inch headspace.
5. Wipe rims with a paper towel moistened with vinegar. Add lids and bands. Hand-tighten.
6. Carefully place jars on rack in canner. Attach and secure canner lid. Heat until

> **Safety Notice**
>
> Do not dredge beef cubes in flour or corn starch before browning since it prevents the heat from penetrating the meat evenly during the canning process. You can add some flour or corn starch when reheating if you prefer a thicker gravy.

canner starts hissing. Allow the steam to escape the vent for 5-10 minutes, add gauge and begin timing after the first jiggle. Process pints for 75 minutes and quarts for 90 minutes at 10 pounds pressure. Adjust timing for higher altitudes.

7. Remove canner from heat. Allow pressure to decrease naturally.
8. Remove lid. Remove jars from the canner after 5 minutes. Cool on a wire rack or kitchen towel. Remove bands, label jars, and store them in a cool, dark place.

# Homestead Prepper Split Pea Soup

Economical and nutritious. Excellent for camping or survival food when you lose power. A fantastic way to use leftover holiday ham.

## INGREDIENTS

- 2 cups dried split peas
- 8 cups water
- 1½ cups sliced t
- 1 cup chopped onion
- 1 cup diced cooked ham
- 1 bay leaf
- ¼ tsp ground allspice
- Canning salt & freshly ground black pepper to taste

## YIELD

5 pints

## Luke's Variations

- I prefer yellow split peas, but you can substitute green split peas if you prefer.
- Don't peel carrots for a more rustic style stew.
- Use petite carrots whole or cut in half depending on size.
- Use 1 cup whole peeled pearl onions instead of chopped onions.
- If you don't have leftover ham, use a ham steak cut into small cubes.

**Luke's Tip:** Use a stick blender to puree the mixture making it as smooth as you wish.

## RECIPE

1. Add peas and water to a large stainless-steel saucepan. Bring to a boil over medium-high heat. Reduce heat, cover, and boil gently for 1 hour.
2. Prepare pressure canner, jars, and lids.
3. Remove from heat and puree peas if a smoother consistency is desired.
4. Add all other ingredients to peas. Bing to boil, stirring often. Reduce heat and simmer gently for 30 minutes stirring often to prevent sticking. After 30 minutes, add boiling water if the soup is too thick. Remove bay leaf.
5. Using a jar funnel, ladle hot soup into hot jars, leaving 1-inch headspace.
6. Wipe rims with a paper towel moistened with vinegar. Add lids and bands to finger tight. Do not overtighten.
7. Carefully place jars on rack in canner. Attach and secure canner lid. Heat until canner starts hissing. Allow the steam to escape the vent for 5-10 minutes, add gauge and begin timing after the first jiggle. Process pints for 75 minutes and quarts for 90 minutes at 10 pounds pressure. Adjust timing for higher altitudes.
8. Remove canner from heat. Allow pressure to decrease naturally.
9. Remove lid. Remove jars from the canner after 5 minutes. Cool on a wire rack or kitchen towel. Remove bands, label jars, and store them in a cool, dark place.

# Classic Tomato Soup

This is a vintage recipe from the 1940s or earlier. The recipe calls for flour and butter, which is not recommended based on modern food safety standards. You can substitute ClearJel for the flour. I also added lemon juice to further acidify the contents.

## INGREDIENTS

- 18 cups peeled, cored, chopped tomatoes
- 2 medium onions peeled and chopped
- 1 stalk celery chopped
- 5 sprigs chopped parsley
- 1 bay leaf
- 4 Tbsp flour (optional)
- 4 Tbsp butter (optional)
- 1 Tbsp canning salt
- 3 Tbsp granulated sugar
- 1 tsp pepper
- 1 tsp lemon juice per pint

## YIELD

Varies

## RECIPE

1. Prepare hot water bath canner, jars, and lids.
2. In a large stainless-steel pot, combine tomatoes, onions, celery, parsley, and bay leaf. Bring to boil over medium-high heat, stirring often to prevent scorching. Reduce heat and simmer for 45 minutes.
3. Remove from heat and pour through a sieve. Discard seeds, onions, celery, and herbs.
4. Melt butter, whisk in flour, or ClearJel, add a little of the hot tomato juice. Whisk until smooth. Add mixture to tomato juice in a large stainless-steel pot. Bring to boil and reduce heat to simmer.
5. Add salt, sugar, and pepper. Mix well. Pour through a sieve again for a smoother consistency.
6. Using a jar funnel, ladle hot soup into hot jars, leaving 1-inch headspace. Add 1 tsp lemon juice to each jar.
7. Wipe rims with a paper towel moistened with vinegar. Add lids and bands to finger tight.
8. Process in a hot water bath for 20 minutes. Adjust timing for higher altitudes.
9. Remove canner from heat. Remove lid. Remove jars from the canner after 5 minutes. Cool on a wire rack or kitchen towel. Remove bands, label jars, and store them in a cool, dark place.

# Italian Bread Soup

Place a slice of toasted garlic-rubbed Italian bread in the bottom of the bowl before serving. Drizzle with extra virgin olive oil and sprinkle with freshly shaved or grated Parmesan cheese for a taste of Tuscany. Mamma Mia!

## INGREDIENTS

- 1 cup dried cannellini beans
- 3 Tbsp extra virgin olive oil
- 1 cup chopped onion
- ½ cup chopped leeks
- ½ cup diced carrots
- ½ cup diced celery
- 1 Tbsp minced garlic
- 1 tsp crushed dried rosemary
- 2 cups peeled, cored, chopped tomatoes
- 2-3 cups cabbage cut into strips
- 2 Tbsp canning salt
- 1 medium peeled, diced potato
- 1 medium sliced zucchini
- 2 cups Swiss chard cut into strips
- Freshly ground black pepper (to taste)

## RECIPE

1. Prepare pressure canner, jars, and lids.
2. Rinse beans under cool water. Place in a large bowl and add 3 cups boiling water. Soak beans for 1 hour. Drain and set aside.
3. Heat olive oil in a large stainless-steel stockpot over medium heat. When hot, add onions, leeks, carrots, and celery. Cook for 3-5 minutes, then add garlic and rosemary. Cook, stirring to prevent scorching, for an additional 2 minutes.
4. Add beans, tomatoes, cabbage, salt, and 8 cups boiling water to stockpot. Bring to a boil over medium-high heat. Reduce heat, cover with a lid and simmer for one hour, occasionally stirring to prevent sticking.

## YIELD

4 quarts

5. Add potatoes, zucchini, and chard. Simmer covered for an additional 30 minutes. Season with canning salt and freshly ground pepper.
6. Using a jar funnel, ladle hot soup into hot jars, leaving 1-inch headspace.
7. Wipe rims of jars with a paper towel moistened with vinegar. Add lids and bands to finger tight.
8. Place jars on rack in canner. Attach and secure canner lid. Heat until canner starts hissing. Allow the steam to escape the vent for 5-10 minutes, add gauge and begin timing after the first jiggle. Process pints and quarts for 90 minutes at 10 pounds pressure. Adjust timing for higher altitudes.
9. Remove canner from heat. Allow pressure to decrease naturally.
10. Remove lid. Remove jars from the canner after 5 minutes. Cool on a wire rack or kitchen towel. Remove bands, label jars, and store them in a cool, dark place.

# Leek and Potato Soup

Add a little cream when reheating to make a cream soup. Sprinkle with toasted croutons or saltines and enjoy!

## INGREDIENTS

- 5 medium potatoes peeled and cubed
- 3-4 cups thinly sliced leeks
- 5 cups vegetable or chicken stock
- Canning salt (to taste)
- Freshly ground black pepper (to taste)

## YIELD

6 pints

## Note

- Refer to the stock recipe in this book. You may also use store-bought stock but it's so easy to make it yourself!

## RECIPE

1. Prepare pressure canner, jars, and lids.
2. Peel and dice potatoes. Rinse under cool water. Slice leeks.
3. Start by layering leeks, then potatoes, then leeks in each jar. Continue layering, leaving 1-inch headspace.
4. Add stock to each jar, leaving 1-inch headspace.
5. Add canning salt and freshly ground pepper to taste to each jar.
6. Wipe rims of jars with a paper towel moistened with vinegar. Add lids and bands to finger tight.
7. Carefully place jars on rack in canner. Attach and secure canner lid. Heat until canner starts hissing. Allow the steam to escape vent for 5-10 minutes, add gauge and begin timing after the first jiggle. Process pints and quarts for 35 minutes at 10 pounds pressure. Adjust timing for higher altitudes.
8. Remove canner from heat. Allow pressure to decrease naturally.
9. Remove lid. Remove jars from the canner after 5 minutes. Cool on a wire rack or kitchen towel. Remove bands, label jars, and store them in a cool, dark place.

# Meatless Spaghetti Sauce with Vegetables

Delicious and super-easy to make! Adjust the recipe based on the pounds of tomatoes you have on hand.

## INGREDIENTS

- 30 lbs fresh tomatoes (plum tomatoes preferred)
- ¼ cup extra virgin olive oil
- 1 cup chopped onion
- 5 garlic cloves peeled
- 1 cup chopped green bell pepper
- 1 lb sliced mushrooms
- 4½ tsp canning salt
- 2 tsp freshly ground black pepper
- 4 Tbsp dried parsley
- 2 Tbsp dried oregano
- 1 Tbsp dried basil
- Red pepper flakes to taste
- ¼ cup packed brown sugar

## YIELD

9 pints

## RECIPE

1. Prepare pressure canner, jars, and lids.
2. Peel and core tomatoes.
3. Cook tomatoes over medium-high heat for 20-30 minutes, stirring often.
4. Add vegetables to tomatoes. Add seasonings. Once the sauce begins to bubble, stir in the brown sugar. Reduce heat and simmer uncovered until the sauce is reduced by about half. Stir often to prevent scorching.
5. Ladle hot sauce into hot jars using a jar funnel, leaving 1-inch headspace.
6. Wipe rims of jars with a paper towel moistened with vinegar. Add lids and bands to finger tight.
7. Carefully place jars on rack in canner. Attach and secure canner lid. Heat until canner starts hissing. Allow the steam to escape vent for 5-10 minutes, add gauge and begin timing after the first jiggle. Process pints and quarts for 20 minutes at 10 pounds pressure. Adjust timing for higher altitudes.
8. Remove canner from heat. Allow pressure to decrease naturally.
9. Remove lid. Remove jars from the canner after 5 minutes. Cool on a wire rack or kitchen towel. Remove bands, label jars, and store them in a cool, dark place.

# Chili con Carne

A crowd pleaser! Top with shredded cheese and hot pepper rings before serving!

## INGREDIENTS

- 3 cups dried red kidney or pinto beans
- 5½ cups water
- 5 tsp canning salt, divided
- 3 lbs ground beef or pork
- 1½ cups chopped onion
- ½-1 cup seeded and chopped pepper of your choice (adjust the amount to your liking)
- 1 tsp freshly ground black pepper
- 3-6 Tbsp chili powder
- 2 quarts peeled, cored tomatoes

## YIELD

9 pints

## RECIPE

1. Prepare pressure canner, jars, and lids.
2. Wash beans thoroughly. Place in a saucepan or a large bowl and add cold water to submerge them. Soak 12-18 hours. Drain beans and rinse again.
3. Peel and core tomatoes.
4. Combine beans with 5½ cups cold water and 2 tsp canning salt. Bring to a boil, reduce heat, and simmer for 30 minutes. Drain.
5. Brown ground meat, onions, and peppers. Drain fat, then add seasonings and tomatoes. Add beans and simmer for 5 minutes.
6. Ladle into hot jars using a jar funnel, leaving 1-inch headspace.
7. Wipe rims of jars with a paper towel moistened with vinegar. Add lids and bands to finger tight.
8. Carefully place jars on rack in canner. Attach and secure canner lid. Heat until canner starts hissing. Allow the steam to escape the vent for 5-10 minutes, add gauge and begin timing after the first jiggle. Process pints and quarts for 75 minutes at 10 pounds pressure. Adjust timing for higher altitudes.
9. Remove canner from heat. Allow pressure to decrease naturally.
10. Remove lid. Remove jars from the canner after 5 minutes. Cool on a wire rack or kitchen towel. Remove bands, label jars, and store them in a cool, dark place.

# Meatless Chili

Perfect for vegetarians and vegans. Serve it at your next Super Bowl party!

## INGREDIENTS

- 3 cups dried red kidney beans
- 1 Tbsp canning salt
- 2 cups chopped onion
- 1 cup diced sweet red bell pepper
- 3 Tbsp chili powder
- 1 tsp freshly ground black pepper
- 8 cups tomato juice
- ½ cup tomato paste
- 2 tsp dried thyme
- 2 tsp ground cumin
- 6 garlic cloves, peeled, minced
- ¼ cup fresh parsley, chopped

## YIELD

9 pints

## RECIPE

1. Add dried kidney beans to a large bowl. Cover with water and soak overnight. In the morning, drain beans, rinse under cool water, and place in a stainless-steel saucepan. Add fresh water and bring to a boil over medium-high heat. Reduce heat and simmer for 30 minutes until beans split in half. Drain well and set aside.
2. Prepare pressure canner, jars, and lids.
3. In a large stainless-steel saucepan, add all ingredients except beans. Bring to a boil over medium-high heat. Add beans and stir thoroughly. Return to a boil. Reduce heat and simmer for 10 minutes.
4. Stir well, ladle hot chili into hot jars using a jar funnel, leaving 1-inch headspace. Remove air bubbles with a rubber spatula, adding more chili if necessary.
5. Wipe rims of jars with a paper towel moistened with vinegar. Add lids and bands to finger tight.
6. Carefully place jars on rack in canner. Attach and secure canner lid. Heat until canner starts hissing. Allow the steam to escape the vent for 5-10 minutes, add gauge and begin timing after the first jiggle. Process pints for 75 minutes at 10 pounds pressure. Adjust timing for higher altitudes.
7. Remove canner from heat. Allow pressure to decrease naturally.
8. Remove lid. Remove jars from the canner after 5 minutes. Cool on a wire rack or kitchen towel. Remove bands, label jars, and store them in a cool, dark place.

# New England Boiled Dinner

Enjoy this traditional taste of St. Patrick's Day any day of the year without all the fuss! Simply reheat and serve!

## INGREDIENTS

- 4-5 lb brisket
- 6 cups white potatoes
- 2 cups carrots
- 1 cup turnips or beets (optional)
- 2-3 onions
- ½ head green cabbage
- Pickling spice
- Freshly ground black pepper
- Water

## YIELD

6-7 quarts

## RECIPE

1. Prepare pressure canner, jars, and lids.
2. Trim as much fat from brisket as possible. Discard fat. Cut brisket into 1-inch chunks.
3. Prepare potatoes and carrots. Cut into 1-inch cubes. Peel and cube turnips or beets. Peel and cut onions into chunks. Slice cabbage into wedges that will fit in your jars.
4. Layer brisket and vegetables into jars, leaving 1-inch headspace.
5. Add ¼ tsp pickling spice to each quart jar. Add freshly ground black pepper to each jar to taste.
6. Add boiling water to each jar, leaving 1-inch headspace.
7. Wipe rims of jars with a paper towel moistened with vinegar. Add lids and bands to finger tight.
8. Carefully place jars on rack in canner. Attach and secure canner lid. Heat until canner starts hissing. Allow the steam to escape vent for 5-10 minutes, add gauge and begin timing after the first jiggle. Process pints for 75 minutes and quarts for 90 minutes at 10 pounds pressure. Adjust timing for higher altitudes.
9. Remove canner from heat. Allow pressure to decrease naturally.
10. Remove lid. Remove jars from the canner after 5 minutes. Cool on a wire rack or kitchen towel. Remove bands, label jars, and store them in a cool, dark place.

# Vegetable Soup

This is a great way to preserve your garden vegetables when they're at their peak!

## INGREDIENTS

- 8 cups peeled, cored, and chopped tomatoes
- 6 cups peeled and diced potatoes
- 6 cups sliced carrots
- 4 cups bush or pole beans cut into 1-inch pieces
- 4 cups corn kernels
- 2 cups chopped celery
- 2 cups chopped onions
- 6 cups water
- 2 tsp canning salt
- 1 tsp freshly ground black pepper
- ½ cup chopped parsley (use much less if using dried)
- 1 Tbsp chopped rosemary (use less if using dried)

## YIELD

7 quarts

## Luke's Variations

Use trimmed, washed, unpeeled baby carrots for a more rustic soup.
Add 3 cloves minced garlic.
Use 3 cups white potatoes and 3 cups sweet potatoes.

## RECIPE

1. Prepare pressure canner, jars, and lids.
2. Combine all prepared vegetables and water in a large stainless-steel pot. Add seasonings and bring to a boil over medium-high heat, stirring often.
3. Reduce heat to medium-low and simmer uncovered for 30 minutes, stirring often.
4. Using a jar funnel, ladle hot soup into hot jars, leaving 1-inch headspace. Remove air bubbles with a rubber spatula and add more soup if needed.
5. Wipe rims of jars with a paper towel moistened with vinegar. Add lids and bands to finger tight.
6. Carefully place jars on rack in canner. Attach and secure canner lid. Heat until canner starts hissing. Allow the steam to escape the vent for 5-10 minutes, add gauge and begin timing after the first jiggle. Process quarts for 85 minutes at 10 pounds pressure. Adjust timing for higher altitudes.
7. Remove canner from heat. Allow pressure to decrease naturally.
8. Remove lid. Remove jars from the canner after 5 minutes. Cool on a wire rack or kitchen towel. Remove bands, label jars, and store them in a cool, dark place.

# JUICES

During WWI, the Great Depression, and WWII, fresh fruits were often unavailable for most of the year. But by canning fruit juices, homemakers were able to add variety to their winter diets. Nowadays, juicing has become commonplace year-round. But modern fruit production is dependent on agribusiness and pesticides, petroleum-based shipping, and preservatives to supply fresh fruit year-round. When you return to the ways of our ancestors, you can have fresh, organic, home-grown fruit juices year-round. If you've never tried canning fruit juices, you're missing out!

# Cranberry Juice

Try serving this with Thanksgiving dinner. Or use it when making your favorite cocktail!

## INGREDIENTS

- 4 cups whole organic cranberries
- 4 cups water
- 2/3 cup granulated sugar

## YIELD

4-5 pints

## RECIPE

1. Prepare hot water bath canner, jars, and lids.
2. Wash and remove any stems from 4 cups organic cranberries. Add to a medium stainless-steel saucepan with 4 cups water.
3. Bring to a boil, reduce heat, and softly boil over medium heat for 15 minutes. Strain juice through a dampened jelly bag or several layers of moistened cheesecloth. Do not squeeze bag.
4. After most of the juice has dripped into a bowl, return the juice to the saucepan, and add sugar, stirring to dissolve. Bring to a boil, then ladle hot juice into hot jars using a jar funnel, leaving ½-inch headspace.
5. Wipe rims with vinegar moistened paper towel. Center lids on jars. Add bands and finger-tighten.
6. Using a jar lifter, carefully place jars in the canner with a rack in place. Make sure they are completely covered with water. Add more boiling water if needed. Cover and return to a boil. Process for 10 minutes.
7. Remove from heat. Remove lid. Wait 5 minutes, then remove jars and place on a wire rack or kitchen towel. Allow to cool, listen for pings, label, and store.

# Spicy Vegetable Juice Cocktail

Add a pickle spear or a celery stalk to make the perfect Bloody Mary or Bloody Maria or drink your vegetables as is!

## INGREDIENTS

- 8 lbs ripe tomatoes
- 1 cup chopped celery
- ½ cup chopped onion
- 6 Tbsp bottled or freshly squeezed lemon juice
- 2 Tbsp granulated sugar
- 1 Tbsp Worcestershire sauce
- 2 tsp prepared horseradish
- 1 tsp canning salt
- Freshly ground black pepper
- ¼ tsp hot sauce (to taste)

## YIELD

4 pints

## RECIPE

1. Prepare hot water bath canner, jars, and lids.
2. Wash tomatoes. Core and remove stem ends. Chop tomatoes and add to a large stainless-steel saucepan.
3. Add celery and onions. Bring to a boil over medium heat, stirring often to prevent scorching. Cover and simmer for about 20 minutes until tomatoes are soft.
4. Pour mixture through a sieve or colander, discarding solids. Measure 12 cups juice and return to saucepan. Bring to a boil, reduce heat and simmer uncovered for 20 minutes. Stir in lemon juice, sugar, Worcestershire sauce, horseradish, salt, pepper, and hot sauce. Return to boiling and simmer uncovered for 15 minutes.
5. Using a jar funnel, ladle hot juice into hot jars, leaving ½-inch headspace.
6. Wipe rims with vinegar moistened paper towel. Center lids on jars. Add bands and finger-tighten.
7. Using a jar lifter, carefully place jars in the canner with a rack in place. Make sure they are completely covered with water. Add more boiling water if needed. Cover and return to a boil. Process for 35 minutes.
8. Remove from heat. Remove lid. Wait 5 minutes, then remove jars and place on a wire rack or kitchen towel. Allow to cool, listen for pings, label, and store.

# Concord Grape Juice

This is an excellent way to preserve an abundant grape harvest.

## INGREDIENTS

- 7-8 lbs Concord grapes
- 2½ cups water
- ½-1 cup granulated sugar (optional)

## YIELD

8 pints

## RECIPE

**Day 1**

1. Wash grapes and remove them from stems. Measure 17 cups of grapes and add them to a large stainless-steel saucepan. Add water, cover, and simmer for 15 minutes, stirring occasionally.
2. Remove from heat and mash grapes using a potato masher. Strain through a damp jelly bag or several damp layers of cheesecloth over a large bowl. Cover and refrigerate for 24 hours which will allow sediment to settle.

**Day 2**

1. Prepare hot water bath canner, jars, and lids.
2. Restrain juice and discard solids. You can strain through a coffee filter, jelly bag, or cheesecloth. Discard sediment.
3. In a large stainless-steel pot, combine grape juice and sugar (optional). Heat to almost boiling, stirring to dissolve the sugar. Remove from heat and skim off any foam that has formed. Discard foam.
4. Using a jar funnel, ladle hot juice into hot jars, leaving ½-inch headspace.
5. Wipe rims with vinegar moistened paper towel. Center lids on jars. Add bands and finger-tighten.
6. Using a jar lifter, carefully place jars in the canner with a rack in place. Make sure they are completely covered with water. Add more boiling water if needed. Cover and bring to a boil. Process for 10 minutes.
7. Remove from heat. Remove lid. Wait 5 minutes, then remove jars and place on a wire rack or kitchen towel. Allow to cool, listen for pings, label, and store.

# Pineapple Juice

Refreshing and perfect for serving with ham at Easter.

## INGREDIENTS

- Pineapples
- Water

## YIELD

Varies

## RECIPE

1. Prepare hot water bath canner, jars, and lids.
2. Peel as many pineapples as you wish to juice. Grind using a food grinder or food processor fitted with a metal blade.
3. Place in a large stainless-steel saucepan adding just enough water to cover. Bring to a boil over medium-high heat, stirring often. Reduce heat to medium and boil softly for 10 minutes.
4. Strain through a damp jelly bag or several damp layers of cheesecloth over a large bowl and using a jar funnel, at once ladle hot juice into hot jars, leaving ½-inch headspace.
5. Wipe rims with vinegar moistened paper towel. Center lids on jars. Add bands and finger-tighten.
6. Using a jar lifter, carefully place jars in the canner with a rack in place. Make sure they are completely covered with water. Add more boiling water if needed. Cover and bring to a boil. Process for 10 minutes.
7. Remove from heat. Remove lid. Wait 5 minutes, then remove jars and place on a wire rack or kitchen towel. Allow to cool, listen for pings, label, and store.

# Grapefruit Juice

Great way to start the day! You've got to move quickly to preserve the fresh taste of the juice, so have everything prepared in advance.

## INGREDIENTS

- Grapefruits

## YIELD

Varies

## RECIPE

1. Prepare hot water bath canner, jars, and lids. Bring water to a boil and keep covered.
2. Wash the grapefruit. Cut in half and extract the juice using a conical-shaped juicer. Strain out seeds and pulp. Move quickly. The quality of the grapefruit juice deteriorates quickly when exposed to air so fill one jar at a time. Leave ½-inch headspace.
3. Wipe rims with vinegar moistened paper towel. Center lids on jars. Add bands and finger-tighten.
4. Using a jar lifter, carefully place jars in the boiling water bath with a rack in place. Make sure they are completely covered with water. Add more boiling water if needed. Cover and return to a boil. Process for 20 minutes.
5. Remove from heat. Remove lid. Wait 5 minutes, then remove jars and place on a wire rack or kitchen towel. Allow to cool, listen for pings, label, and store.

# Apple Juice

A tasty way to keep the doctor away!

## INGREDIENTS

- 24 lbs apples, stemmed and chopped
- 8 cups water

## YIELD

12 pints

## RECIPE

1. Prepare apples by combining apples with water in a large stainless-steel saucepan. Bring to a boil over medium-high heat. Reduce heat and boil gently, stirring often, until apples are soft.
2. Strain through a damp jelly bag or several damp layers of cheesecloth over a large bowl. Allow to drip for 2-3 hours. Do not squeeze bag.
3. Prepare hot water bath canner, jars, and lids.
4. Return juice to a large stainless-steel saucepan. Heat over medium heat until almost boiling. Maintain juice at this temperature for 5 minutes.
5. Using a jar funnel, ladle hot juice into hot jars, leaving ½-inch headspace.
6. Wipe rims with vinegar moistened paper towel. Center lids on jars. Add bands and finger-tighten.
7. Using a jar lifter, carefully place jars in the canner with a rack in place. Make sure they are completely covered with boiling water. Add more boiling water if needed. Cover and return to a boil. Process for 10 minutes.
8. Remove from heat. Remove lid. Wait 5 minutes, then remove jars and place on a wire rack or kitchen towel. Allow to cool, listen for pings, label, and store.

# FRUITS

Before modern transportation and refrigeration, fresh fruit was available seasonally. Homemakers canned their harvests when fresh fruit was in season to enjoy the taste and health benefits all year long.

# Fruit Cocktail

Traditionally, a delicious treat in the middle of winter when fresh fruits weren't available.

## INGREDIENTS

- 5¼ cups light syrup*
- 1 pineapple
- 3 lbs peaches
- 3 lbs pears
- 1 lb fresh cherries
- 1 lb seedless grapes, any variety

## YIELD

9 pints

## RECIPE

1. Prepare light syrup. Keep hot but not boiling.
2. Prepare hot water bath canner, jars, and lids.
3. Prepare the pineapple by slicing off the bottom and the green top. Slice off the skin and discard. Remove eyes with a sharp paring knife. Cut pineapple in half lengthwise and then cut each half in half again. Slice off and discard core from each quarter. Cut pineapple into bite-sized chunks. Measure 3 cups and set aside.
4. Peel, pit, and cut peaches into similar-sized chunks. Measure 8½ cups peaches. Set aside.
5. Peel, core, and cut pears into chunks. Measure 6½ cups pears. Immerse pear chunks into a bowl of lemon water until ready to use to reduce discoloration.
6. Cut cherries in half and discard pits. Measure 2½ cups cherries. Set aside.
7. Remove the stems from grapes. Keep whole. Measure 3 cups grapes. Set aside.
8. In a large stainless-steel pot, add all fruits. Add hot light syrup and bring to a boil over medium-high heat, stirring often.
9. Immediately, ladle hot fruits and light syrup into hot jars using a jar funnel. Leave ½-inch headspace. Add more syrup as needed leaving ½-inch headspace. Wipe rims of jars with a paper towel dipped in vinegar.

10. Center lids on jars. Add bands and finger-tighten.
11. Using a jar lifter, carefully place jars in the canner with a rack in place. Make sure they are completely covered with water. Add more boiling water if needed. Cover and bring to a boil. Process for 20 minutes.
12. Remove from heat. Remove lid. Wait 5 minutes, then remove jars and place on a wire rack or kitchen towel. Allow to cool, listen for pings, label, and store.

**\*Light Syrup Recipe**

Dissolve 1¼ cups granulated sugar in 5 cups water. Heat over medium heat until sugar dissolves.

# Whole Berry Cranberry Sauce

Easy to make and so much better than store-bought. When you make it ahead of time, it's one less thing to worry about on Thanksgiving Day! It also makes a thoughtful gift if you're invited to someone's home for Thanksgiving or Christmas dinner.

## INGREDIENTS

- 4 cups granulated sugar
- 4 cups water
- 8 cups fresh cranberries

## YIELD

4 pints

## Luke's Variation

Add the grated zest of one orange to the sauce during the last few minutes of cooking.

## RECIPE

1. Prepare hot water bath canner, jars, and lids.
2. In a large stainless-steel saucepan, combine sugar and water. Bring to a boil over high heat, stirring to dissolve sugar. Boil hard for 5 minutes.
3. Rinse cranberries under cool water and remove any stems. Add to boiling sugar/water mixture and return to a boil. Reduce heat and boil gently. Stir occasionally until all berries burst. This should take about 15 minutes.
4. Immediately ladle hot sauce into hot jars using a jar funnel. Leave ¼-inch headspace. Remove air bubbles with a rubber spatula. Wipe rims of jars with a paper towel dipped in vinegar.
5. Center lids on jars. Add bands and finger-tighten.
6. Using a jar lifter, carefully place jars in the canner with a rack in place. Make sure they are completely covered with water. Add more boiling water if needed. Cover and bring to a boil. Process for 15 minutes.
7. Remove from heat. Remove lid. Wait 5 minutes, then remove jars and place on a wire rack or kitchen towel. Allow to cool, listen for pings, label, and store.

# Applesauce

In addition to apple cider, dried apples, and apple butter, this is a traditional way to preserve your apple harvest so it lasts all year! Although you can make applesauce from any variety of apples, my favorites for this recipe are McIntosh and Rome Beauty.

## INGREDIENTS

- 8 lbs cooking apples, cored and quartered
- 2 cups water
- ¼ cup freshly squeezed lemon juice
- 1 cup granulated sugar

## YIELD

6 pints

## RECIPE

1. Prepare hot water bath canner, jars, and lids.
2. In a large stainless-steel saucepan, combine prepared apples, water, and lemon juice. Bring to a boil over medium-high heat, stirring to prevent scorching. Reduce heat to medium-low and simmer covered for 30 minutes until apples are tender, stirring often.
3. Press apples through a sieve or food mill to remove skins and seeds over a large bowl. Return pulp to pan, add sugar, stirring to dissolve and return to a boil. Add more boiling water, if necessary, to achieve desired consistency.
4. Immediately, ladle hot applesauce into hot jars using a jar funnel. Leave ½-inch headspace. Remove air bubbles with a rubber spatula. Wipe rims of jars with a paper towel dipped in vinegar.

5. Center lids on jars. Add bands and finger-tighten.
6. Using a jar lifter, carefully place jars in the canner with a rack in place. Make sure they are completely covered with water. Add more boiling water if needed. Cover and bring to a boil. Process pints for 15 minutes and quarts for 20 minutes.
7. Remove from heat. Remove lid. Wait 5 minutes, then remove jars and place on a wire rack or kitchen towel. Allow to cool, listen for pings, label, and store.

**Cinnamon and Brown Sugar Applesauce**

In Step 2, add 2 broken cinnamon sticks to apples. Simmer as directed. Remove sticks before pressing through the sieve. Replace granulated sugar with ¾ cup dark brown sugar.

# Perfect Peaches

Enjoy this delightful taste of summer all year long! Serve with freshly whipped cream.

### INGREDIENTS

- Fresh peaches
- Ascorbic acid
- Light syrup*

### YIELD

1-1½ pounds of fresh peaches per pint

### RECIPE

1. Prepare hot water bath canner, jars, and lids.
2. Immerse whole peaches in boiling water for 1 minute. Remove with a slotted spoon and immerse peaches in ice water. Skins should slip off easily. Halve and pit peaches. Slice into wedges if desired. Treat with ascorbic acid to prevent browning. (See note below.)
3. In a large stainless-steel saucepan, combine peaches and light syrup. Bring to a boil over medium-high heat, stirring to prevent scorching.
4. Immediately, ladle hot peaches and syrup into hot jars using a jar funnel. Leave ½-inch headspace. Remove air bubbles with a rubber spatula. Add more syrup if necessary, leaving ½-inch headspace.
5. Wipe rims of jars with a paper towel dipped in vinegar.
6. Center lids on jars. Add bands and finger-tighten.

7. Using a jar lifter, carefully place jars in the canner with a rack in place. Make sure they are completely covered with water. Add more boiling if needed. Cover and bring to a boil. Process pints for 20 minutes and quarts for 25 minutes.
8. Remove from heat. Remove lid. Wait 5 minutes, then remove jars and place on a wire rack or kitchen towel. Allow to cool, listen for pings, label, and store.

**Note**

Ascorbic acid can be found in most markets and stores that stock canning supplies. Follow package directions to prevent the browning of fruits during the canning process like peaches and apples.

**\*Light Syrup Recipe**

Dissolve 1¼ cups granulated sugar in 5 cups water. Heat over medium heat until sugar dissolves.

# Blueberries

Follow the same steps to can currants, elderberries, gooseberries, and huckleberries.

## INGREDIENTS

- Blueberries
- Light syrup*

## YIELD

1-3 pounds of berries for each quart

## RECIPE

1. Prepare hot water bath canner, jars, and lids.
2. Immerse blueberries in hot but not boiling water and simmer for 30 seconds. Drain.
3. Fills jars with berries and hot syrup, leaving ½-inch headspace.
4. Wipe rims of jars with a paper towel dipped in vinegar.
5. Center lids on jars. Add bands and finger-tighten.
6. Using a jar lifter, carefully place jars in the canner with a rack in place. Make sure they are completely covered with water. Add more boiling water if needed. Cover and bring to a boil. Process both pints and quarts for 15 minutes.
7. Remove from heat. Remove lid. Wait 5 minutes, then remove jars and place on a wire rack or kitchen towel. Allow to cool, listen for pings, label, and store.

*Light Syrup Recipe

Dissolve 1¼ cups granulated sugar in 5 cups water. Heat over medium heat until sugar dissolves.

# Pears

Select just ripe, unblemished pears with no soft or mushy spots.

## INGREDIENTS

- Fresh pears
- Ascorbic acid
- Light syrup*

## YIELD

2-3 pounds of fresh pears per quart

## RECIPE

1. Prepare hot water bath canner, jars, and lids.
2. Peel, halve, and core pears. Treat with ascorbic acid to prevent browning. Drain and set aside.
3. In a large stainless-steel saucepan, prepare light syrup over medium heat. When sugar is completely dissolved, add pear halves and simmer uncovered for 5 minutes.
4. Immediately, ladle hot pears and syrup into hot jars using a jar funnel. Leave ½-inch headspace. Remove air bubbles with a rubber spatula. Add more syrup if necessary, leaving ½-inch headspace.
5. Wipe rims of jars with a paper towel dipped in vinegar.
6. 6. Center lids on jars. Add bands and finger-tighten.
7. Using a jar lifter, carefully place jars in the canner with a rack in place. Make sure they are completely covered with water. Add more boiling water if needed. Cover and bring to a boil. Process pints for 20 minutes and quarts for 25 minutes.
8. Remove from heat. Remove lid. Wait 5 minutes, then remove jars and place on a wire rack or kitchen towel. Allow to cool, listen for pings, label, and store.

**Note**

Ascorbic acid can be found in most markets and stores that stock canning supplies. Follow package directions to prevent the browning of fruits during the canning process like peaches and apples.

**\*Light Syrup Recipe**

Dissolve 1¼ cups granulated sugar in 5 cups water. Heat over medium heat until sugar dissolves.

# Old-Fashioned Red Cinnamon Apples
## Just like great-grandma used to make!

### INGREDIENTS

- Apples
- Cinnamon
- Red food coloring
- Light syrup*

### YIELD

Varies

### RECIPE

1. Prepare hot water bath canner, jars, and lids.
2. Prepare the light syrup in a large stainless-steel saucepan. Flavor the syrup with cinnamon to taste and add a few drops of red food coloring. Keep syrup warm while preparing apples.
3. Peel and core apples. Cut into quarters and add to warm syrup as you complete each apple.
4. When all apples have been added to the syrup, bring to a boil over medium-high heat. Reduce heat and cook for 3-5 minutes.
5. Using a jar funnel, ladle hot apples and syrup into hot jars. Leave ½-inch headspace. Remove air bubbles with a rubber spatula. Add more syrup if necessary, leaving ½-inch headspace.
6. Wipe rims of jars with a paper towel dipped in vinegar.
7. Center lids on jars. Add bands and finger-tighten.
8. Using a jar lifter, carefully place jars in a boiling water bath. Make sure they are completely covered with water. Add more boiling water if needed. Cover and return to a boil. Process pints for 25 minutes.

9. Remove from heat. Remove lid. Wait 5 minutes, then remove jars and place on a wire rack or kitchen towel. Allow to cool, listen for pings, label, and store.

**\*Light Syrup Recipe**

Dissolve 1¼ cups granulated sugar in 5 cups water. Heat over medium heat until sugar dissolves.

# PIE FILLINGS

The next time you want to make a pie or turnover, you simply have to make the pastry crust and fill!

# Easy as Apple Pie Filling
The taste of home!

## INGREDIENTS

- 1 lemon
- 10-12 lbs apples (about 24)
- 5½ cups granulated sugar
- 1½ cups ClearJel
- 1 Tbsp cinnamon
- ½ tsp nutmeg
- ¼ tsp ground cloves
- 5 cups apple juice
- 2½ cups cold water
- ¾ cup lemon juice

## YIELD

7 quarts

## RECIPE

1. Prepare hot water bath canner, lids, and jars.
2. Fill 2 large bowls with cold water and add half the juice of 1 lemon to each.
3. Peel, core, and cut apples into wedges. Immediately immerse apple pieces into the lemon water to prevent browning.
4. Drain the apples reserving the lemon water. In a stainless-steel saucepan, bring the lemon water to a boil. Measure 24 cups apples. Working in batches, add the apples to boiling water, cooking 1 minute per batch. Remove cooked apples with a slotted spoon to a large bowl. Cover with a cloth to keep the apples hot.
5. When apples are done, drain the saucepan. Add sugar, ClearJel, and spices. Stir in apple juice and 2½ cups cold water. Bring to a boil over medium-high heat, stirring constantly until the mixture begins to thicken. Add lemon juice and boil for 1 more minute. Stir in apples.

6. Using a jar funnel, ladle hot filling into hot, sterilized jars leaving about 1-inch headspace.
7. Wipe down rims of jars with a paper towel moistened with vinegar.
8. Add lids and bands to finger tight.
9. Carefully place jars on rack in canner. Cover and return to a boil. Process quarts for 25 minutes.
10. Remove canner from heat. Remove cover. After 5 minutes, remove jars from the canner using a jar lifter. Cool on a wire rack or kitchen towel. Remove bands, label jars, and store them in a cool, dark place.

**Note**

The best apples for this recipe include Honey Crisp, Golden Delicious, Gaia, and Granny Smith.

# Mom's Strawberry Rhubarb Pie Filling

A family favorite in my home for many generations – sweet and tart!

## INGREDIENTS

- 3 large apples
- 1 Tbsp grated orange rind
- ¼ cup freshly squeezed orange juice
- 7 cups sliced rhubarb
- 2 cups granulated sugar
- 4 cups strawberries

## YIELD

5 pints

## RECIPE

1. Prepare hot water bath canner, lids, and jars.
2. In a large stainless-steel saucepan, combine apples, peeled, and diced, orange zest, and orange juice. Stir to coat apples. Stir in rhubarb sliced in 1-inch pieces and sugar. Bring to a boil over medium-high heat, stirring often to prevent scorching. Reduce heat and boil gently for about 15 minutes until rhubarb is tender. Add hulled, halved strawberries and their juice and return to a boil. Remove from heat.
3. Using a jar funnel, ladle hot pie filling into hot, sterilized jars leaving about 1-inch headspace. Remove air bubbles with a rubber spatula.
4. Wipe down rims of jars with a paper towel moistened with vinegar.
5. Add lids and bands to finger tight.
6. Carefully place jars on rack in canner. Cover and return to a boil. Process quarts for 15 minutes.
7. Remove canner from heat. Remove cover. After 5 minutes, remove jars from the canner using a jar lifter. Cool on a wire rack or kitchen towel. Remove bands, label jars, and store them in a cool, dark place.

**Note**

I suggest cooking apples such as Granny Smith, Rome Beauty, or Golden Delicious.

# Blueberry Pie Filling

*Serve at a summer picnic or family reunion!*

## INGREDIENTS

- 3 quarts water
- 8 quarts fresh blueberries
- 8 cups granulated sugar
- 3 cups ClearJel
- 9 cups cold water
- 2/3 cup lemon juice

## YIELD

7 quarts

## RECIPE

1. Prepare hot water bath canner, lids, and jars.
2. Rinse and drain blueberries under cool water. Remove any remaining stems. In a large stainless-steel saucepan, bring 3 quarts of water to a boil. Working in batches, add 8 cups of blueberries at a time to the boiling water for 30 seconds. Remove berries with a slotted spoon to a large bowl.
3. When finished, drain the pot, and add sugar and ClearJel. Add 9 cups cold water, stirring until dry ingredients dissolve. Bring to a boil over medium-high heat, stirring constantly. Add lemon juice and boil for 1 more minute. Remove from heat. Add blueberries all at once and stir to coat.
4. Using a jar funnel, ladle hot filling into hot, sterilized jars leaving about 1-inch headspace.
5. Wipe down rims of jars with a paper towel moistened with vinegar.
6. Add lids and bands to finger tight.
7. Carefully place jars on rack in canner. Cover and return to a boil. Process quarts for 30 minutes.
8. Remove canner from heat. Remove cover. After 5 minutes, remove jars from the canner using a jar lifter. Cool on a wire rack or kitchen towel. Remove bands, label jars, and store them in a cool, dark place.

# Meatless Mincemeat Pie Filling

Perfect fruity filling for pies, cookies, and tarts. And vegan-friendly!

## INGREDIENTS

- 6 cups apples
- 1 large lemon
- 2 medium oranges
- 4 cups seedless raisins*
- 2 cups currants
- 4 tsp cinnamon
- 1½ tsp nutmeg
- 1½ tsp ground cloves
- 1½ tsp allspice
- 1 tsp canning salt
- 3-4 Tbsp ClearJel
- ½ cup granulated sugar
- 6 Tbsp unsweetened applesauce
- 3 tsp rum extract (optional)

## YIELD

4 pints

## RECIPE

1. Quarter and core apples. Do not peel. Grind in an old-fashioned food grinder using the medium-coarse blade. Set aside in a large ceramic or glass bowl.
2. Quarter lemon and oranges. Remove all seeds but leaves rinds intact. Grind and add to ground apples.
3. Grind 2 cups of raisins and add to bowl.
4. Add the rest of the raisins (whole) and all other ingredients to the bowl. Stir well. Cover and refrigerate for 1 week.
5. After 1 week, prepare jars, lids, and hot water bath canner.
6. Heat pie filling until hot but not boiling over medium-low heat, stirring often.
7. Using a jar funnel, ladle heated pie filling into hot, sterilized jars leaving ½-inch headspace. Remove air bubbles with a rubber spatula.
8. Wipe down rims of jars with a paper towel moistened with vinegar.
9. Add lids and bands to finger tight.
10. Carefully place jars on rack in canner. Cover and return to a boil. Process pints for 20 minutes, adjusting for altitude.
11. Remove canner from heat. Remove cover. After 5 minutes, remove jars from the canner using a jar lifter. Cool on a wire rack or kitchen towel. Remove bands, label jars, and store them in a cool, dark place.

*You can use 2 cups regular seedless raisins and 2 cups golden raisins, also known as sultana raisins, if you prefer.

# Old-Fashioned Green Tomato Mincemeat Pie Filling

This is a vintage recipe using beef suet.

## INGREDIENTS

- 1½ pints chopped tart apples
- 1 pint chopped green tomatoes
- 2 tsp cinnamon
- 1 tsp canning salt
- 1 tsp allspice
- 1 tsp ground cloves
- 3 cups granulated sugar
- 1 lb raisins*
- ¼ cup vinegar
- 1 cup chopped beef suet

## YIELD

Uncertain because my grandma didn't specify on her recipe card!

## RECIPE

1. Prepare hot water bath canner, jars, and lids.
2. Peel, core, and chop apples.
3. Mix all ingredients in a large stainless-steel saucepan. Bring all ingredients to a boil over medium-high heat, stirring constantly. Reduce heat to medium-low and simmer until thick, stirring often.
4. Using a jar funnel, ladle heated pie filling into hot, sterilized jars leaving ½-inch headspace. Remove air bubbles with a rubber spatula.
5. Wipe down rims of jars with a paper towel moistened with vinegar.
6. Add lids and bands to finger tight.
7. Carefully place jars on rack in canner. Cover and return to a boil. Process pints and quarts for 25 minutes, adjusting for altitude.
8. Remove canner from heat. Remove cover. After 5 minutes, remove jars from the canner using a jar lifter. Cool on a wire rack or kitchen towel. Remove bands, label jars, and store them in a cool, dark place.

*You can use one-half pound regular seedless raisins and one-half pound golden raisins, also known as sultana raisins, if you prefer.

# Peach Pie Filling

It makes a great pie or cobbler!

## INGREDIENTS

- 1 cinnamon stick broken in half
- 2 tsp whole cloves
- 12 cups peeled, pitted, sliced peaches
- 2 cups peeled, cored, finely chopped apples
- 2 2/3 cups granulated sugar
- 1 cup seedless golden raisins
- 2 Tbsp grated lemon zest
- ½ cup lemon juice
- ¼ cup white vinegar
- ½ tsp ground nutmeg

## YIELD

4 pints

## RECIPE

1. Prepare hot water bath canner, jars, and lids.
2. Create a spice bag by tying cinnamon and cloves in a cheesecloth square.
3. Mix all ingredients in a large stainless-steel saucepan. Bring all ingredients to a boil over medium-high heat, stirring constantly. Cover and reduce heat to medium-low and simmer, stirring often, until thickened. Remove spice bag.
4. Using a jar funnel, ladle hot pie filling into hot, sterilized jars leaving 1-inch headspace. Remove air bubbles with a rubber spatula.
5. Wipe down rims of jars with a paper towel moistened with vinegar.
6. Add lids and bands to finger tight.
7. Carefully place jars on rack in canner. Cover and return to a boil. Process for 15 minutes, adjusting for altitude.
8. Remove canner from heat. Remove cover. After 5 minutes, remove jars from the canner using a jar lifter. Cool on a wire rack or kitchen towel. Remove bands, label jars, and store them in a cool, dark place.

# Pumpkin or Squash Pie Filling

Use in place of store-bought pumpkin or squash pie filling to finish off your Thanksgiving dinner in style!

## INGREDIENTS

- 10 lbs pumpkin or 10 lbs acorn, Hubbard, or butternut squash

## YIELD

6 pints

## RECIPE

1. Prepare pressure canner, jars, and lids.
2. Cut pumpkin or squash into medium size chunks. Peel and discard peels.
3. Add chunks to a stainless-steel saucepan with just enough water to cover. Bring to a boil over medium-high heat, then lower heat to medium and cook, covered, until fork-tender.
4. Drain liquid and process in a food processor fitted with a metal blade until smooth.
5. Using a jar funnel, fill jars leaving ½-inch headspace. Remove air bubbles with a rubber spatula.
6. Wipe down rims of jars with a paper towel moistened with vinegar.
7. Add lids and bands to finger tight.
8. Place jars on rack in canner. Attach and secure canner lid. Heat until canner starts hissing. Allow the steam to escape the vent for 5-10 minutes, add gauge and begin timing after the first jiggle. Cover and process at 10 pounds pressure for 15 minutes after first jiggle adjusting for altitude.
9. Remove canner from heat. After pressure drops, remove the lid. After 5 minutes, remove jars from the canner using a jar lifter. Cool on a wire rack or kitchen towel. Remove bands, label jars, and store them in a cool, dark place.

> **Luke's Suggestion**
>
> I prefer the taste and flavor of squash pie over pumpkin pie. Try it if you've never had it, and you'll never go back!

> **FYI**
>
> All pumpkins are members of the squash family, but not all squash are pumpkins. Pumpkins are round, thick-skinned squash. The more you know.

**To Make Pie**

1. Empty 1 pint canned pumpkin or squash into a large mixing bowl.
2. Mix ¾ cup granulated sugar, 1 tsp cinnamon, ½ tsp salt, ½ tsp ground ginger, ¼ tsp ground cloves in a separate bowl. Then stir into filling.
3. Beat 2 eggs slightly. Stir well into the filling.
4. Gradually add 1 12oz can evaporated milk stirring until filling is smooth.
5. Pour pie filling into 9-inch unbaked 1 crust pie shell. Bake at 425 degrees for 15 minutes, then reduce heat to 350 degrees and bake 40-45 minutes until a knife inserted comes out clean.
6. Cool on a wire rack for several hours. Serve with whipped cream.

# VEGETABLES

Bursting with nutrients, canning your home-gown vegetables is easy and the results are delicious!

# Ma's Classic Green Beans

There's an old black and white picture taken of me in 1958 when I was 2 years old, hoeing beans in the family vegetable garden. Over 60 years later, and I'm still at it! This family recipe preserves the classic taste of green beans and becomes the main ingredient for the perfect green bean casserole for Thanksgiving!

## INGREDIENTS

- Beans
- Canning salt (optional)

## YIELD

Varies

## Luke's Variations

You can use any variety or color of string bean, bush bean, or pole bean for this recipe.

## RECIPE

1. Harvest and rinse freshly gathered young, tender, crisp beans under cold running water. Drain.
2. Trim ends. Leave whole or cut into 2-inch pieces.
3. Pack tightly into hot, sterilized jars leaving about 1-inch headspace.
4. Add ½ tsp of canning salt to each pint jar.
5. Add boiling water to each jar, leaving 1-inch headspace.
6. Add lids and bands. Hand-tighten.
7. Carefully place jars on rack in pressure canner. Attach and secure canner lid. Heat until canner starts hissing, then add

vent and begin timing. Process pints for 20 minutes and quarts for 25 minutes at 10 pounds pressure. Adjust timing for higher altitudes.
8. Remove canner from heat. Allow pressure to decrease naturally.
9. Remove lid. Remove jars from the canner after 5 minutes. Cool on a wire rack or kitchen towel. Remove bands, label jars, and store them in a cool, dark place.

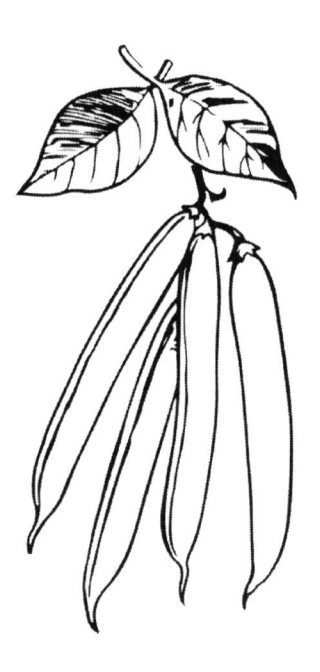

# Stewed Tomatoes and Vegetables

Because this recipe calls for low acid vegetables, it must be processed in a pressure canner. My mom served this as a vegetable side dish and added a dab of butter to each bowl before serving us. Add to casseroles!

## INGREDIENTS

- 16 cups peeled, cored, chopped tomatoes (any types)
- 1 cup celery
- ½ cup chopped onion (any type)
- ¼ cup chopped seeded green bell pepper
- 1 Tbsp granulated sugar
- 2 tsp canning salt
- Freshly ground black pepper to taste
- Bottled lemon juice

## YIELD

7 pints

## Luke's Variation

To easily peel tomatoes, score an X on the bottom of each tomato using a sharp knife. Drop them in a pot of boiling water for 60 seconds. Remove with a slotted spoon and drop them in ice water. The peels will then slide off easily!

## RECIPE

1. In a large stainless-steel saucepan, add tomatoes, celery, onion, green pepper, sugar, salt, and pepper. Bring to a gentle boil over medium heat, stirring often to prevent sticking. Cover and boil gently for about 10 minutes.
2. Add 1 tsp lemon juice to each pint jar to acidify the contents.
3. Pack hot tomato/vegetable mixture into hot jars using a slotted spoon, leaving 1-inch headspace. Add juice from the saucepan to cover. Using a rubber spatula, remove air bubbles. Wipe rims with a paper towel soaked in vinegar. Center lids, add bands, and finger-tighten.
4. Using a jar lifter, gently place jars in the pressure canner. Adjust water level if necessary and lock lid. Bring to boil until steam escapes, vent for 5-10 minutes, add gauge, and process jars at 10 pounds pressure for 15 minutes.
5. Turn off heat and allow pressure to return to zero. Remove lid, wait 10 minutes, then remove from canner. Cool, label, and store jars.

# Vintage Stewed Tomatoes and Vegetables

Back in the day, instead of using a pressure canner, homemakers simply processed low acid foods for a longer processing time in a hot water bath. This recipe calls for the vegetables to be raw packed instead of precooked. I added lemon juice to the recipe to further acidify the contents.

## INGREDIENTS

- 8 cups peeled cored tomatoes cut into chunks
- 4 Tbsp chopped green pepper
- 4 Tbsp chopped onion
- 8 Tbsp chopped celery
- 2 tsp celery salt
- 2 tsp sugar
- ½ tsp canning salt
- Bottled lemon juice

## YIELD

6-7 pints

## RECIPE

1. Measure all vegetables after chopping and mix in a large bowl.
2. Pack into sterilized jars leaving ½-inch headspace.
3. Add 1 tsp lemon juice to each pint jar to further acidify the contents.
4. Using a rubber spatula, remove air bubbles. Wipe rims with a paper towel moistened with vinegar. Center lids, add bands, and finger-tighten.
5. Process in boiling water bath for 45 minutes.
6. Remove canner from heat. Remove lid, wait 10 minutes, then remove jars from canner. Cool, label, and store jars.

# Whole Kernel Corn

Enjoy the taste of summer all year long! Warm up with some butter, and salt, and it's like eating corn on the cob! Or use in soups, shepherd's pie, casseroles, add to a salad, etc.

## INGREDIENTS

- 12 ears corn, shucked with kernels removed
- Canning salt

## YIELD

6 8oz jars

## RECIPE

1. Shuck corn, remove silks.
2. Using a knife or corn cob stripper or cutter, remove kernels from the cob.
3. Add kernels to clean, hot jars leaving 1-inch headspace.
4. Add ¼ tsp canning salt to each 8oz jar or ½ tsp to a pint jar.
5. Add boiling water to each jar leaving 1-inch headspace.
6. Wipe rims, add lids and bands.
7. Place jars on rack in canner. Attach and secure canner lid. Heat until canner starts hissing. Allow the steam to escape the vent for 5-10 minutes, add gauge and begin timing after the first jiggle. Process at 10 pounds pressure for 55 minutes for 8oz jars and pints, 85 minutes for quart jars.
8. Turn off heat and allow pressure to return to zero. Remove lid, wait 10 minutes, then remove from canner. Cool, label, and store jars.

# Easy Creamed Corn

New England favorite! You'll need about 4 ears of corn for each pint.

## INGREDIENTS

- 12 ears corn
- Canning salt (optional)

## YIELD

3 pints

## RECIPE

1. Shuck corn, remove silks, wash ears.
2. Blanch ears in a large pot of boiling water for 3-5 minutes.
3. Using a serrated knife or corn cob stripper, remove kernels from the cob.
4. Scrape cobs with a knife to extract pulp and milk.
5. Add kernels, pulp, and milk to a large bowl. Measure. For every 2 cups corn mixture, add 1 cup boiling water.
6. Add to a large stainless-steel saucepan, bring to boil, reduce heat and boil gently for 3 minutes.
7. Ladle mixture into pint jars, leaving 1-inch headspace. Add ½ tsp canning salt to each jar if desired.
8. Wipe rims, add lids and bands.
9. Place jars on rack in canner. Attach and secure canner lid. Heat until canner starts hissing. Allow the steam to escape the vent for 5-10 minutes, add gauge and begin timing after the first jiggle. Process pints for 85 minutes at 10 pounds pressure.
10. Turn off heat and allow pressure to return to zero. Remove lid, wait 10 minutes, then remove from canner. Cool, label, and store jars.

# Green Peas

Fresh home-canned green peas are far superior to their supermarket counterpart.

## INGREDIENTS

- Sweet green peas
- Canning salt (optional)

## YIELD

2¼ lbs pea pods for each pint jar

## Luke's Variations

Follow the same steps and process for the exact time for black-eyed peas, field peas, or crowder peas.

## RECIPE

1. Select plump, young pea pods. Rinse under cold water. Shell,
2. rinse peas again.
3. Loosely fill jars with peas leaving 1-inch headspace.
4. Add ½ tsp canning salt to each pint jar.
5. Add boiling water to each jar, leaving 1-inch headspace.
6. Wipe rims, add lids and bands.
7. Place jars on rack in canner. Attach and secure canner lid. Heat until canner starts hissing. Allow the steam to escape the vent for 5-10 minutes, add gauge and begin timing after the first jiggle. Process 40 minutes at 10 pounds pressure for both pint and quart jars.
8. Turn off heat and allow pressure to return to zero. Remove lid, wait 10 minutes, then remove from canner. Cool, label, and store jars.

# Winter Squash

Use Blue Hubbard, acorn, or butternut squash. Do not use summer squash.

## INGREDIENTS

- Winter squash
- Boiling water
- Canning salt (optional)

## YIELD

2¼ lbs squash for each quart jar

## RECIPE

1. Prepare pressure canner, jars, and lids.
2. Peel and cut the squash into chunks. Place in a stainless-steel saucepan. Add enough water to cover and bring to a boil over medium-high heat. Boil for 2 minutes. Do not overcook.
3. Drain and discard cooking water. Add squash to jars leaving 1-inch headspace. Add boiling water to cover, leaving 1-inch headspace. Add ½ tsp canning salt if desired.
4. Wipe rims, add lids and bands.
5. Place jars on rack in canner. Attach and secure canner lid. Heat until canner starts hissing. Allow the steam to escape the vent for 5-10 minutes, add gauge and begin timing after the first jiggle. Process pints for 55 minutes and quarts for 90 minutes at 10 pounds pressure adjusting for altitude. Turn off heat and allow pressure to return to zero. Remove lid, wait 10 minutes, then remove jars from canner using a jar lifter. Cool, label, and store jars.

# Carrots

Just drain the liquid and warm the carrots up with some butter and salt for a delicious side dish!

## INGREDIENTS

- Carrots
- Canning salt (optional)

## YIELD

1-1½ lbs of carrots for each pint jar

## RECIPE

1. Wash carrots. Peel and wash again.
2. Leave small carrots whole or slice or dice larger carrots.
3. Pack carrots into hot jars, leaving 1-inch headspace.
4. Add ½ tsp canning salt to each pint jar.
5. Add boiling water to each jar, leaving 1-inch headspace.
6. Wipe rims, add lids and bands.
7. Place jars on rack in canner. Attach and secure canner lid. Heat until canner starts hissing. Allow the steam to escape the vent for 5-10 minutes, add gauge and begin timing after the first jiggle. Process pints for 25 minutes at 10 pounds pressure.
8. Turn off heat and allow pressure to return to zero. Remove lid, wait 10 minutes, then remove from canner. Cool, remove bands, label, and store jars.

# Greens

This recipe works for all leafy greens, including beet, Swiss chard, spinach, mustard, kale, and collard greens.

## INGREDIENTS

- Leafy greens
- Canning salt (optional)

## YIELD

2 lbs of fresh, tender leaves for each pint jar

## RECIPE

1. Wash greens well in several changes of cold water. Trim and discard tough stems.
2. In a large stainless-steel pot of boiling water, add greens, 1 pound at a time until they wilt.
3. Drain greens and chop on a cutting board. Fill jars leaving 1-inch headspace.
4. Add ½ tsp canning salt to each pint jar.
5. Add boiling water to each jar leaving 1-inch headspace.
6. Wipe rims, add lids and bands.
7. Place jars on rack in canner. Attach and secure canner lid. Heat until canner starts hissing. Allow the steam to escape the vent for 5-10 minutes, add gauge and begin timing after the first jiggle. Process pints for 70 minutes at 10 pounds pressure adjusting for altitude.
8. Turn off heat and allow pressure to return to zero. Remove lid, wait 10 minutes, then remove from canner. Cool, remove bands, label, and store jars.

# Beets

*This traditional recipe is quick and easy to prepare.*

## INGREDIENTS

- Beets
- Granulated sugar
- Canning salt

## YIELD

1-1½ pounds of beets for each pint jar

## RECIPE

1. To prepare beets, leave the roots and two inches stem intact. Scrub thoroughly to remove dirt. Place in a saucepan and bring to boil. Reduce heat and cook until tender. Remove beets and run under cold water. Slip off the skins, remove stem, and taproot. Leave small beets whole or slice or quarter larger beets.
2. Prepare canner, jars, and lids.
3. Add prepared beets to hot jars leaving 1-inch headspace. Add 1 tsp canning salt and 1 tsp granulated sugar to each jar. Add boiling water to each jar, leaving 1-inch headspace.
4. Wipe rims with a paper towel moistened with vinegar. Add lids and bands to finger tight.
5. Place jars on rack in canner. Attach and secure canner lid. Heat until canner starts hissing. Allow the steam to escape the vent for 5-10 minutes, add gauge and begin timing after the first jiggle. Process pints for 30 minutes at 10 pounds pressure.
6. Turn off heat and allow pressure to return to zero. Remove lid, wait 10 minutes, then remove from canner. Cool, remove bands, label, and store jars.

# Okra

Use only small, crisp, brightly colored pods.

## INGREDIENTS

- Okra
- Canning salt (optional)

## YIELD

¾-1 pound of okra for each pint jar

## RECIPE

1. To prepare okra, wash, and drain. Remove stem and blossom ends without cutting into the pods. Leave whole or cut into 1-inch slices.
2. Add okra and hot water to a stainless-steel saucepan. Bring to a boil over medium-high heat and boil for 2 minutes. Drain and discard cooking liquid.
3. Add hot okra to hot jars leaving 1-inch headspace. Add ½ tsp canning salt to each jar (optional). Pour boiling water into each jar, leaving 1-inch headspace.
4. Wipe rims with a paper towel moistened with vinegar. Add lids and bands to finger tight. Add jars to pressure canner.
5. Place jars on rack in canner. Attach and secure canner lid. Heat until canner starts hissing. Allow the steam to escape the vent for 5-10 minutes, add gauge and begin timing after the first jiggle. Process pints for 25 minutes and quarts for 40 minutes at 10 pounds pressure.
6. Turn off heat and allow pressure to return to zero. Remove lid, wait 10 minutes, then remove from canner. Cool, remove bands, label, and store jars.

# Sweet Potatoes

What would Thanksgiving be without sweet potato casserole or sweet potato pie?

## INGREDIENTS

- Sweet Potatoes
- Boiling water
- Canning salt (optional)

## YIELD

2½ lbs sweet potatoes for each quart jar

## RECIPE

1. Prepare pressure canner, jars, and lids.
2. Wash and boil sweet potatoes for 15-20 minutes. Cool slightly. Remove skins and cut them into uniform-sized chunks.
3. Pack into hot jars, leaving 1-inch headspace. Add boiling water to cover, leaving 1-inch headspace. Add ½ tsp canning salt per jar if desired.
4. Wipe rims, add lids and bands.
5. Place jars on rack in canner. Attach and secure canner lid. Heat until canner starts hissing. Allow the steam to escape the vent for 5-10 minutes, add gauge and begin timing after the first jiggle. Process pints for 65 minutes and quarts for 90 minutes at 10 pounds pressure adjusting for altitude. Turn off heat and allow pressure to return to zero. Remove lid, wait 10 minutes, then remove jars from canner using a jar lifter. Cool, label, and store jars.

# White, Red and Yellow Potatoes

Warm up, drain, add butter, salt, pepper, and mash. Delicious!

## INGREDIENTS

- Potatoes
- Boiling water
- Canning salt (optional)

## YIELD

2½ lbs potatoes for each quart jar

## RECIPE

1. Prepare pressure canner, jars, and lids.
2. Wash potatoes. Peel and wash again. Leave small potatoes whole. Cut larger potatoes into uniform chunks. Place in a stainless-steel saucepan. Add enough water to cover and bring to a boil over medium-high heat. Boil for 5-10 minutes. Do not overcook.
3. Drain and discard cooking water. Add potatoes to jars leaving 1-inch headspace. Add boiling water to cover, leaving 1-inch headspace. Add ½ tsp canning salt to each jar.
4. Wipe rims, add lids and bands. Using a jar lifter, place in a pressure canner. Process pints for 35 minutes and quarts for 40 minutes at 10 pounds pressure adjusting for altitude. Turn off heat and allow pressure to return to zero. Remove lid, wait 10 minutes, then remove jars from canner using a jar lifter. Cool, label, and store jars.

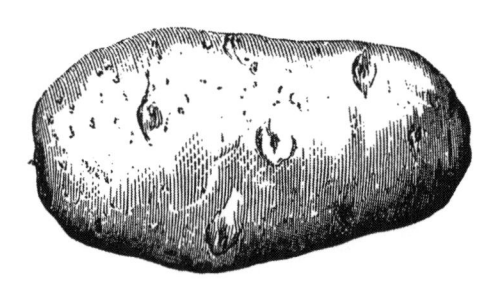

# JELLIES, JAMS, FRUIT BUTTERS & MARMALADES

Canning jelly is fun and easy! You'll create beautiful, canned goods in every shade of the rainbow! You can make mouth-watering jellies out of fruits, juices, vegetables, and even herbs and flowers. Jelly, unlike jams and preserves, is clear and firm when sliced. Most jelly recipes require the addition of pectin for the liquid to gel. Jellies make colorful gifts!

# Concord Grape Jelly

Use a combination of fully ripe and slightly under-ripe Concord grapes for the best results.

## INGREDIENTS

- 3½-4 lbs Concord grapes
- ½ cup water
- 6¾ cups granulated sugar
- 1 3oz pouch liquid pectin

## YIELD

7 8oz jars

## RECIPE

1. Wash grapes and remove stems. Crush grapes, one cup at a time in a large stainless-steel saucepan. Add water. Bring to a boil over medium-high heat. Reduce heat and simmer, covered, for about 10 minutes.

2. Using a damp jelly bag or colander lined with several layers of moistened food-grade cheesecloth, pour cooked grapes and juice into a jelly bag or colander. Let drain for about 2 hours. Do not squeeze bag or cheesecloth. Measure 4 cups of prepared grape juice into a large bowl. Cover and refrigerate the juice for 12-24 hours.

3. Strain chilled juice through a damp jelly bag or colander lined with moistened cheesecloth a second time. Place juice in a large stainless-steel saucepan. Add sugar all at once. Bring to a full rolling boil over medium-high heat, stirring often to prevent scorching. When the mixture cannot be stirred down, add liquid pectin all at once. Boil hard for 1 minute, stirring constantly. Remove from heat and skim off foam with a large spoon. Discard foam.

4. Immediately ladle hot jelly into hot jars using a jar funnel. Leave ¼-inch headspace. Wipe rims of jars with a paper towel dipped in vinegar.

5. Center lids on jars. Add bands and finger-tighten.
6. Using a jar lifter, carefully place jars in a hot water bath canner with a rack in place. Make sure they are completely covered with water. Add more boiling water if needed. Add lid and return to a boil. Process for 10 minutes, adjusting for altitude.
7. Remove from heat. Remove lid. Wait 5 minutes, then remove jars and place on a wire rack or kitchen towel. Allow to cool, listen for pings, label, and store.

# Granny's Apple Jelly

First, make apple juice from fresh apples, any variety, or a mixture. Then, make your jelly!

## INGREDIENTS

- 5-6 lbs apples
- 1 package 1.75oz regular powdered fruit pectin
- 7 cups granulated sugar

## YIELD

7 8oz jars

## RECIPE

**Prepare Apple Juice**

1. Wash apples. Remove stem and blossom ends. Place quartered apples, skin, and core intact in a large stainless-steel saucepan. Add about 5 cups cold water. Bring to a boil over high heat, stirring often. Reduce heat and simmer, covered loosely, for about 30 minutes until apples are soft.
2. Remove from heat. Crush apples slightly using a potato masher.
3. Transfer apple pulp and juice to a dampened jelly bag or a colander lined with several layers of dampened cheesecloth over a deep bowl. Let drip for 4 hours or overnight. Do not squeeze bag or cheesecloth.

**Making Jelly**

1. Prepare hot water bath canner, lids, and jars.
2. In a deep stainless-steel saucepan, add apple juice. Whisk in pectin until thoroughly dissolved. Bring to a boil over high heat, stirring often to prevent scorching. Add sugar all at once and return to a full rolling boil stirring constantly. Boil hard for about 1 minute. Remove from heat and quickly skim off foam with a large spoon. Discard foam.

3. Immediately ladle hot jelly into hot jars using a jar funnel. Leave ¼-inch headspace. Wipe rims of jars with a paper towel dipped in vinegar.
4. Center lids on jars. Add bands and finger-tighten.
5. Using a jar lifter, carefully place jars in the canner with a rack in place. Make sure they are completely covered with water. Add more boiling water if needed. Cover and bring to a boil. Process for 10 minutes.
6. Remove from heat. Remove lid. Wait 5 minutes, then remove jars and place on a wire rack or kitchen towel. Allow to cool, listen for pings, label, and store.

**Crabapple Jelly**

Use 5-6 lbs crabapples in place of regular apples to make the apple juice. Follow all other steps

# Rose Hip Jelly

Collect the hips from wild beach roses after the first frost to make this old-fashioned sweet and tart favorite.

## INGREDIENTS

- 2 quarts rose hips
- 6 cups water
- ½ cup freshly squeezed lemon juice
- 1 1.75oz package regular powdered pectin
- ½ tsp butter to reduce foaming
- 3½ cups granulated sugar

## YIELD

5 8oz jars

## RECIPE

1. Rinse rose hips. Remove stem end. Place in a large stainless-steel pot and add 6 cups water. Bring to a boil, then reduce heat and simmer covered for 1 hour.
2. Using a potato masher, mash the rose hips into a pulp. Transfer pulp and juice to a dampened jelly bag or a colander lined with several layers of dampened cheesecloth over a deep bowl. Let drip for 1-2 hours until you have 3 cups strained juice. Do not squeeze bag or cheesecloth.
3. Prepare hot water bath canner, lids, and jars.
4. Add 3 cups of rose hip juice, lemon juice, and powdered pectin to a deep stainless-steel saucepan. Whisk in the pectin until thoroughly dissolved. Add the sugar all at once, stirring to dissolve. Then add the butter (optional). Bring to a full rolling boil stirring constantly. Boil hard for 1 minute. Remove from heat and quickly skim off foam with a large spoon. Discard foam.
5. Immediately ladle hot jelly into hot jars using a jar funnel. Leave ¼-inch headspace. Wipe rims of jars with a paper towel dipped in vinegar.
6. Center lids on jars. Add bands and finger-tighten.

7. Using a jar lifter, carefully place jars in the canner with a rack in place. Make sure they are completely covered with water. Add more boiling water if needed. Cover and bring to a boil. Process for 10 minutes.
8. Remove from heat. Remove lid. Wait 5 minutes, then remove jars and place on a wire rack or kitchen towel. Allow to cool, listen for pings, label, and store.

# Fresh Blueberry Jelly

First, make blueberry juice from fresh blueberries. Include some slightly under-ripe berries to enhance natural pectin content. Discard over-ripe, mushy berries. Then, make your jelly!

## INGREDIENTS

- 2 quarts fresh blueberries
- 4 cups water
- 2 pouches 3oz each liquid pectin
- 12 cups granulated sugar

## YIELD

12 8oz jars

## RECIPE

1. Place blueberries in a large stainless-steel pot. Crush berries using a potato masher. Add water and bring to a boil over medium-high heat, stirring often. Reduce heat to medium and cook, uncovered, for 45 minutes. Line a colander with four layers of moistened cheesecloth and place over a bowl or use a moistened jelly bag with a stand. Place pulp and liquid in colander or jelly bag. Let drip for 1 hour or until you have 6 cups of blueberry juice.

2. Pour juice back into the pot. Gradually stir in sugar until it dissolves. Bring to a boil over high heat, stirring constantly. Stir in pectin. Bring to a rolling boil that cannot be stirred down and stir constantly for 1 minute.

3. Remove from heat and quickly skim off foam with a large spoon. Discard foam.
4. Immediately ladle hot jelly into hot jars using a jar funnel. Leave ¼-inch headspace. Wipe rims of jars with a paper towel dipped in vinegar.
5. Center lids on jars. Add bands and finger-tighten.
6. Using a jar lifter, carefully place jars in a hot water bath canner with a rack in place. Make sure they are completely covered with water. Add more boiling water if needed. Cover and return to a boil. Process for 5 minutes.
7. Remove from heat. Remove lid. Wait 5 minutes, then remove jars and place on a wire rack or kitchen towel. Allow to cool, listen for pings, label, and store.

# Strawberry Jelly

You'll get more juice from your strawberries if you freeze them for 24-48 hours. Thaw in the refrigerator, then mash and pour in a jelly bag.

## INGREDIENTS

- 4-5 quarts fresh strawberries
- 1 1.75oz package regular powdered fruit pectin
- 4½ cups granulated sugar
- ½ tsp butter (to reduce foaming)

## YIELD

5 8oz jars

## RECIPE

1. Place thawed strawberries in a large stainless-steel pot. Crush berries using a potato masher. Line a colander with four layers of moistened cheesecloth and place over a bowl or use a moistened jelly bag with a stand. Pour pulp and liquid into the colander or jelly bag. Let drip for 2-4 hours or until you have 3½ cups of strawberry juice.
2. Pour juice back into the pot. Whisk in powdered pectin and butter. Bring to a boil over medium-high heat, stirring often. Add sugar all at once and return to a rolling boil that cannot be stirred down. Boil hard, stirring constantly for 1 minute.
3. Remove from heat and quickly skim off foam with a large spoon. Discard foam.
4. Immediately ladle hot jelly into hot jars using a jar funnel. Leave ¼-inch headspace. Wipe rims of jars with a paper towel dipped in vinegar.
5. Center lids on jars. Add bands and finger-tighten.
6. Using a jar lifter, carefully place jars in a hot water bath canner with a rack in place. Make sure they are completely covered with water. Add more boiling water if needed. Cover and return to a boil. Process for 10 minutes.
7. Remove from heat. Remove lid. Wait 5 minutes, then remove jars and place on a wire rack or kitchen towel. Allow to cool, listen for pings, label, and store.

# Hot Sriracha Pepper Jelly

Hot and sweet! Serve it with crackers, cheese, and fruits at your next party.

## INGREDIENTS

- 12oz sriracha peppers (about 8-10)
- 2 cups apple cider vinegar
- 6 cups sugar
- 2 3oz pouches liquid pectin
- Green food coloring (optional)

## YIELD

5 8oz jars

## RECIPE

1. Remove stems. Place peppers and 1 cup apple cider vinegar in a food processor or blender. Puree.
2. Add 6 cups sugar and 1 cup apple cider vinegar to a large stainless-steel pot. Add pureed pepper mixture. Add a few drops of green food coloring if desired. Stir well.
3. Bring to boil over high heat. Boil hard for 10 minutes. Stir often.
4. Add 2 pouches of liquid pectin all at once. Stir and return to a full boil. Stir constantly for 1 minute.
5. Remove from heat and skim off foam. Discard foam. Using a jar funnel, pour into jars leaving ¼-inch headspace. Wipe rims, add lids and bands to finger tight.
6. Using a jar lifter, place jars in a hot water bath canner. Cover. Return to a full boil. Process for 10 minutes.
7. Remove pot from heat source. Remove cover. After 5 minutes, remove jars to cooling rack or towel.
8. Cool, label, and store jars.

**Banana Pepper Jelly:** Use 12oz yellow banana peppers instead of sriracha peppers. Use a few drops of yellow food coloring if desired.

**Hot Hungarian Pepper Jelly:** Use 12oz Hungarian wax peppers instead of sriracha peppers.

**Jalapeno Jelly:** Use 12oz jalapeno peppers instead of sriracha peppers.
Or mix and match any combination of peppers using 12oz total.

# Fresh Herb Jelly

Not all jellies are sweet. Savory jellies can be served with cheese and crackers or as a glaze for meat, poultry, or fish.

## INGREDIENTS

- 2 cups coarsely chopped parsley, basil, thyme, dill, or any combination of fresh herbs
- 1½ cups unsweetened apple juice
- 1 cup water
- 1 cup white wine vinegar
- 1 1.75oz package powdered pectin
- 5¼ cups granulated sugar
- Food coloring (optional)

## YIELD

5 8oz jars

## Luke's Variations

Add a few drops of green food coloring to the jelly mixture when it is cooking.

## Note

Using white wine vinegar allows the flavor of the herbs to take center stage.

## RECIPE

1. Combine herbs, apple juice, water, and vinegar in a large stainless-steel saucepan. Bring to a boil over medium heat. Remove from heat, cover, and let steep for 30 minutes. Stir, pressing down on herbs to extract flavor and oils.
2. Transfer herbs and liquid to a moistened jelly bag or strain through several layers of damp cheesecloth into a large bowl. Let drip for 30 minutes or longer. Do not squeeze bag.
3. Prepare hot water bath canner, jars, and lids.
4. Transfer strained juice to a large stainless-steel saucepan. Whisk in powdered pectin until fully dissolved. Bring to a bowl over medium-high heat, stirring often. When boiling, add sugar all at once, stirring constantly to dissolve. When mixture reaches a full rolling boil, time for 1 minute stirring constantly. Remove from heat and skim off foam. Discard foam.
5. Using a jar funnel, pour hot jelly into hot jars, leaving ¼-inch headspace. Wipe rims with a paper towel moistened with vinegar. Add lids and bands to finger tight.
6. Using a jar lifter, place jars in a boiling water bath. Cover. Return to a full boil. Process for 10 minutes.
7. Remove canner from heat. Remove cover. After 5 minutes, remove jars to cooling rack or towel.
8. Cool, label, and store jars.

# Lemon and Lavender Jelly

Make this in the summer when your herb garden is in bloom!

## INGREDIENTS

- 3-4 lemons
- 1 1/3 cups boiling water
- 2 Tbsp fresh just-opened lavender flowers (or 1 Tbsp dried lavender flowers crushed)
- 4¼ cups granulated sugar
- 1 3oz pouch liquid pectin

## YIELD

4 8oz jars

## RECIPE

1. Remove 2 Tbsp lemon zest. Squeeze ¾ cup juice from the lemons. In a large glass bowl, add zest, lemon juice, lavender flowers, and boiling water. Cover with a cloth and let stand 1 hour.
2. Prepare hot water bath canner, jars, and lids.
3. Strain mixture through a fine sieve. Discard peel, pulp, and flowers.
4. Transfer strained liquid to a large stainless-steel saucepan. Add the sugar and bring to a full boil over high heat, stirring constantly. Stir in liquid pectin and return to a full rolling boil that cannot be stirred down. Boil hard for 1 minute, stirring constantly.
5. Remove from heat and skim off foam. Discard foam.
6. Using a jar funnel, pour hot jelly into hot jars, leaving ¼-inch headspace. Wipe rims with a paper towel moistened with vinegar. Add lids and bands to finger tight.
7. Using a jar lifter, place jars in a boiling water bath. Cover. Return to a full boil. Process for 5 minutes.
8. Remove canner from heat. Remove cover. After 5 minutes, remove jars to cooling rack or towel.
9. Cool, label, and store jars.

# Patten's Farm Stand Strawberry Jam

In the late 1970s, my first job was on a strawberry farm. I earned 7 cents a quart for picking strawberries. A few summers later, the pay was increased to 10 cents a quart. One day I picked 100 quarts which meant I earned $10 for 8+ hours in the hot, summer sun. But it was worth it because earning my own money allowed me to buy a tape recorder, record albums, and my own school clothes. While working on the farm, I learned how to make this mouth-watering strawberry jam from the berries I had just picked. Your whole family will love this delicious, fresh-tasting jam. The taste of nostalgia!

## INGREDIENTS

- 3¾ cups crushed hulled strawberries
- 4 Tbsp lemon juice
- 7 cups granulated sugar
- 1 tsp butter (to reduce foaming)
- 1 3oz pouch liquid pectin

## YIELD

8 8oz jars

## RECIPE

1. In a large, deep pan, combine crushed strawberries and their juice, lemon juice, and sugar. Add butter. Stir constantly over high heat until it comes to a full rolling boil that cannot be stirred down. Stir in pectin all at once. Return to a rolling boil and boil hard, stirring constantly for 1 minute. Remove from heat.
2. Skim foam off the surface with a large spoon. Discard foam. Your liquid should be clear with pieces of fruit.
3. Ladle hot jam into hot jars. Leave ¼-inch headspace. Wipe down rims of jars with a paper towel dipped in vinegar.
4. Center lids on jars. Add bands and finger-tighten.
5. Using a jar lifter, carefully place jars in a hot water bath canner with a rack in place. Make sure they are completely covered with water. Add more boiling water if needed. Add lid and bring to a boil. Process for 10 minutes.
6. Remove from heat. Remove lid. Wait 5 minutes, then remove jars and place them on a kitchen towel or wire rack. Allow to cool, listen for pings, label, and store.

# Blueberry Jam

Not everyone has a garden or a farm. But you can still preserve the taste of summer all year long when you buy fresh ingredients from a local farm stand or pick-your-own. This recipe is simple and delicious!

## INGREDIENTS

- 4½ cups crushed blueberries (about 3 pints)
- ¼ cup lemon juice
- 7 cups granulated sugar
- 1 tsp butter
- 2 3oz pouches liquid pectin

## YIELD

8 8oz jars

## RECIPE

1. In a large, deep stainless-steel pan, combine crushed blueberries and their juice, lemon juice, and sugar. Add butter. Stir constantly over high heat until it comes to a full rolling boil that cannot be stirred down. Stir in pectin all at once. Boil hard, stirring constantly for 1 minute. Remove from heat.
2. Skim foam off the surface with a large spoon. Discard foam. Your liquid should be clear with pieces of fruit.
3. Ladle hot jam into hot jars. Leave ¼-inch headspace. Wipe down rims of jars with a paper towel dipped in vinegar.
4. Center lids on jars. Add bands and finger-tighten.
5. Using a jar lifter, carefully place jars in a hot water bath canner with a rack in place. Make sure they are completely covered with water. Add more boiling water if needed. Add lid and bring to a boil. Process for 10 minutes.
6. Remove from heat. Remove lid. Wait 5 minutes, then remove jars and place them on a kitchen towel or wire rack. Allow to cool, listen for pings, label, and store.

# Triple Berry Jam

An easy jam made without pectin combining the flavors and colors of 3 summer fruit favorites!

## INGREDIENTS

- 3 cups cut-up strawberries
- 1½ cups blueberries
- 1½ cups raspberries
- ¾ cup granulated sugar
- Zest of 1 lemon
- 2 tsp lemon juice
- 1 tsp butter

## YIELD

3-4 8oz jars

## RECIPE

1. In a large bowl, combine all 3 fruits and sugar. Stir together and allow to sit for 1-2 hours until sugar is dissolved and syrupy.
2. Add mixture to a stainless-steel saucepan and bring to a boil over medium-high heat, stirring often. Reduce heat to medium-low and boil gently for 30-40 minutes until the jam begins to thicken. Mash fruits with a potato masher, then stir in butter, lemon zest and lemon juice. Cook for 5 more minutes. Remove from heat.
3. Skim foam off the surface with a large spoon. Discard foam. Your liquid should be clear with pieces of fruit.
4. Ladle hot jam into hot jars. Leave ¼-inch headspace. Wipe down rims of jars with a paper towel dipped in vinegar.
5. Center lids on jars. Add bands and finger-tighten.
6. Using a jar lifter, carefully place jars in a hot water bath canner with a rack in place. Make sure they are completely covered with water. Add more boiling water if needed. Add the lid and bring to a boil. Process for 10 minutes.
7. Remove from heat. Remove lid. Wait 5 minutes, then remove jars and place them on a kitchen towel or wire rack. Allow to cool, listen for pings, label, and store.

# Raspberry Jam

If you want fewer seeds in your raspberry jam, press half or more of the crushed berries through a sieve and discard the seeds.

## INGREDIENTS

- 12 cups fresh raspberries
- 1 1.75oz package powdered fruit pectin
- ½ tsp butter (optional)
- 7 cups granulated sugar

## YIELD

8 8oz jars

## RECIPE

1. Crush raspberries, one cup at a time, in a large stainless-steel saucepan. Continue crushing until you have 5 cups of crushed berries.
2. Stir in pectin and butter (optional) and bring to a full rolling boil that cannot be stirred down, stirring constantly. Once you have reached the rolling boil, time for exactly 1 minute. Remove from heat and skim the foam off the surface with a large spoon. Discard foam.
3. Immediately, ladle hot jam into hot jars. Leave ¼-inch headspace. Wipe down rims of jars with a paper towel dipped in vinegar.
4. Center lids on jars. Add bands and finger-tighten.
5. Using a jar lifter, carefully place jars in a hot water bath canner with a rack in place. Make sure they are completely covered with water. Add more boiling water if needed. Add lid and bring to a boil. Process for 10 minutes.
6. Remove from heat. Remove lid. Wait 5 minutes, then remove jars and place on a wire rack or kitchen towel. Allow to cool, listen for pings, label, and store.

# Queen's Jam

This Scandinavian favorite is served on Swedish pancakes and drizzled over ice cream!

## INGREDIENTS

- 2 pints fresh raspberries
- 1 pint fresh blueberries
- 1¾ cups granulated sugar
- Juice of one-half lemon

## YIELD

3-4 8oz jars

## RECIPE

1. Layer raspberries and blueberries in a large stainless-steel saucepan. Crush with a potato masher. Add the sugar, stir well to dissolve the sugar, and let sit for 30 minutes.
2. Add lemon juice. Bring to a full rolling boil that cannot be stirred down, stirring often. Once the jam reaches 220 degrees, remove from heat, and skim the foam off the surface with a large spoon. Discard foam and, at once, ladle hot jam into hot jars. Leave ¼-inch headspace. Wipe down rims of jars with a paper towel dipped in vinegar.
3. Center lids on jars. Add bands and finger-tighten.
4. Using a jar lifter, carefully place jars in a hot water bath canner with a rack in place. Make sure they are completely covered with water. Add more boiling water if needed. Cover and bring to a boil. Process for 20 minutes.
5. Remove from heat. Remove lid. Wait 5 minutes, then remove jars and place on a wire rack or kitchen towel. Allow to cool, listen for pings, label, and store.

# New England Apple Cider Butter

Apple butter, cider, and applesauce were old-timey ways of preserving the apple harvest. It wasn't too many generations ago that fall was the only time you could get apples. I suggest using one or a combination of the following varieties if you have a choice: Red Delicious, Yellow Delicious, or Rome.

## INGREDIENTS

- 6 lbs apples, peeled, cored, and quartered
- 2 cups apple cider
- 3 cups granulated sugar
- 1½ tsp ground cinnamon
- ½ tsp ground cloves
- ½ tsp ground nutmeg

## YIELD

Makes about 4 pints

## RECIPE

1. Prepare hot water bath canner, jars, and lids.
2. Mix sugar and spices. Set aside.
3. In a large stainless-steel saucepan, combine apples and apple cider. Bring to a boil over medium-high heat. Reduce heat and boil gently for 30 minutes, stirring occasionally until apples are soft.
4. Cool slightly, then puree apples in a food processor or grinder until smooth. Do not liquefy.
5. Measure 12 cups of apple puree into a large stainless-steel pot. Add sugar/spice mixture and stir until sugar is dissolved. Bring to a boil over medium-high heat, stirring often to prevent scorching. Reduce heat and boil gently until the mixture holds its shape on a spoon.

### Luke's Variations

Substitute 1 cup local honey for the 3 cups of sugar. This recipe will be slightly less sweet.

### Traditional Apple Butter

Replace apple cider with 3 cups water. Increase sugar to 5 cups.

6. Immediately ladle hot butter into hot jars using a jar funnel. Leave ¼-inch headspace. Wipe rims of jars with a paper towel dipped in vinegar.
7. Center lids on jars. Add bands and finger-tighten.
8. Using a jar lifter, carefully place jars in a hot water bath canner with a rack in place. Make sure they are completely covered with water. Add more boiling water if needed. Cover and bring to a boil. Process for 10 minutes.
9. Remove from heat. Remove lid. Wait 5 minutes, then remove jars and place on a wire rack or kitchen towel. Allow to cool, listen for pings, label, and store.

# Traditional Orange Marmalade

This old-fashioned marmalade recipe has been a family favorite since WWII, when oranges were considered a delicacy in most of the United States.

## INGREDIENTS

- 4 oranges (2 cups)
- 3 lemons (1½ cups)
- Granulated sugar

## YIELD

Use 8oz or smaller jars

## RECIPE

1. Chop oranges and lemons, including rinds, into small chunks. Place in a large bowl and add 6 cups cold water. Cover with a cloth and let sit overnight.
2. Add water and fruit to a large stainless-steel saucepan. Bring to a boil over medium-high heat, stirring often. Reduce heat to medium-low and cook for about 30 minutes until fruits are tender. Remove from heat. Cover and let sit overnight.
3. On the third day, prepare hot water bath canner, jars, and lids.
4. Measure fruit bits and juice. Add to a large stainless-steel saucepan. For each 16oz, add 2 cups granulated sugar stirring as you go to dissolve the sugar.
5. Heat mixture to jelly stage*, about 10 minutes. Remove from heat and skim off foam. Using a jar funnel, pour hot marmalade into hot jars, leaving ¼-inch headspace.

6. Wipe rims, add lids and bands to finger tight.
7. Process in a hot water bath canner for 5 minutes.**
8. Using a jar lifter, remove jars and cool on a wire rack or kitchen towel. Remove bands, label, and store.

*Jelly stage is achieved when the jelly mixture drips off a spoon in a "sheet." The temperature of the jelly should be 220-222 degrees.

**Old recipes don't call for the use of a hot water bath. Home canners usually sealed the jars with paraffin and lids, and the temperature of the hot marmalade was typically enough to seal the jars. Although some still employ this method, it is no longer considered safe by modern food safety standards.

# Old-Fashioned Carrot and Orange Marmalade

This old-fashioned marmalade recipe does not call for processing in a hot water bath, but I've added it to meet modern food safety standards. Since these old recipes don't use liquid or powdered pectin, they require a longer cooking time.

## INGREDIENTS

- 2 cups uncooked ground carrots
- 1 orange
- 2 lemons
- Granulated sugar
- 3 cups water

## YIELD

Use 8oz or smaller jars

## RECIPE

1. Prepare hot water bath canner, jars, and lids.
2. Squeeze and extract the juice from the oranges and lemons. Set aside. Grind the rinds using a food grinder or food processor. Add the ground rinds to a large stainless-steel saucepan. Add just enough water to cover. Cook over medium heat for about 30 minutes until tender, stirring often to prevent scorching. Add the ground carrots, stir to blend, and cook an additional 30 minutes. Add the orange and lemon juice. Remove from heat.
3. Measure the mixture and add an equal amount of water. Remeasure. For each cup of this mixture, add 2/3 cup granulated sugar.
4. Return to clean stainless-steel saucepan and bring to a boil over high heat, stirring often, until mixture reaches the jelly stage*. This will take about an hour.
5. Remove from heat and skim off foam. Discard foam. Using a jar funnel, pour hot marmalade into hot jars, leaving ¼-inch headspace.
6. Wipe rims, add lids and bands to finger tight.
7. Process in a hot water bath canner for 5 minutes.

8. Using a jar lifter, remove jars and cool on a wire rack or kitchen towel. Remove bands, label, and store.

*Jelly stage is achieved when the jelly mixture drips off a spoon in a "sheet." The temperature of the jelly should be 220-222 degrees.

# Strawberry Lemon Marmalade

Try this instead of syrup on pancakes and waffles!

## INGREDIENTS

- 2 lemons
- ½ cup water
- 1/8 tsp baking soda
- 6 cups strawberries (3 cups when crushed)
- 5 cups granulated sugar
- 1 3oz package liquid pectin

## YIELD

Makes about 6 8oz jars

## RECIPE

1. Prepare hot water bath canner, jars, and lids.
2. Wash and peel the lemons. Set the peeled lemons aside. Scrape off the inner white part of the rind and discard. Slice the lemon peels into very thin strips.
3. In a large stainless-steel saucepan, combine lemon peels, water, and baking soda. Bring to a boil, reduce heat and simmer covered for 20 minutes. Chop lemons, reserving juice, discard seeds, and add lemons and juice to the saucepan. Add crushed strawberries and return to boiling. Reduce heat and simmer covered for 10 minutes.
4. Add sugar all at once. Return to a full, rolling boil stirring constantly. Stir in liquid pectin and return to a full, rolling boil that cannot be stirred down. Boil hard for 1 minute, stirring constantly. Remove from heat and quickly skim off foam. Using a jar funnel, pour hot marmalade into hot jars, leaving ¼-inch headspace.
5. Wipe rims, add lids and bands to finger tight.
6. Process in a hot water bath canner for 5 minutes.
7. Using a jar lifter, remove jars and cool on a wire rack or kitchen towel. Remove bands, label, and store for 2 weeks before serving.

# PICKLES & PICKLED VEGETABLES

Pickling began more than 4000 years ago when ancient Mesopotamians began preserving cucumbers in brine to preserve them. We're still enjoying them today!

# Grammie's Victory Garden Dill Pickles

This traditional family recipe has been used successfully for 100 years with excellent results! My family never processes the pickles in a hot water bath, and the boiling brine is typically sufficient to seal the lids. But you can process them for 5 minutes in a hot water bath for added peace of mind.

## INGREDIENTS

- 2 quarts hot water
- 1 quart white vinegar
- ¾ cup canning salt
- Fresh dill or dill seed
- Garlic cloves
- Peppercorns
- Pickling cucumbers, sliced

## YIELD

Makes 6-8 pints

## Luke's Secret to Crisper Pickles

Soak cucumber slices in a bowl of salted ice water.

Remove blossom end.

Do not use English cucumbers.

Use right from the garden cucumbers that are not too large, old, mushy, or seedy.

Add 1/8 teaspoon Ball Pickle Crisp Granules to each pint jar before processing. This is calcium chloride and helps make crisp, delicious pickles every time!

## RECIPE

1. Prepare hot water bath canner, jars, and lids.
2. Mix 2 quarts of hot water and 1 quart white vinegar in a stainless-steel saucepan. Add ¾ cup canning salt. Bring to a hard boil which cannot be stirred down.
3. Add your cucumber slices to clean hot canning jars. Do not pack them down and leave some headspace for the liquid to be added.
4. Add dill flowers, leaves, stems, or dill seed to each jar. Add one peeled garlic clove to each jar. Add a few whole black peppercorns to each jar.

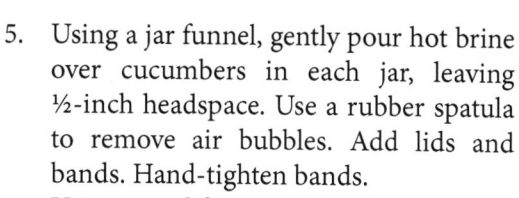

5. Using a jar funnel, gently pour hot brine over cucumbers in each jar, leaving ½-inch headspace. Use a rubber spatula to remove air bubbles. Add lids and bands. Hand-tighten bands.
6. Using a jar lifter, carefully place each jar in a boiling hot water bath. Make sure the jars are not crowded and are covered with water. Add more boiling water if needed. Cover pot and return to a boil.
7. Process for 5 minutes. Remove from the heat and remove the lid. Wait another 5 minutes, and then using a jar lifter, place each jar upright on a towel or wire rack. Allow to cool completely. Although you could eat these pickles immediately, I suggest waiting a week or two to allow the flavors to develop fully. Be sure to label each jar with what it holds and the date it was canned for long-term storage. Before storing, remove the bands. Do not stack the jars on top of each other.

# Old-Fashioned Cucumber and Onion Pickles

My maternal grandmother was born in Canada, and her family brought this traditional recipe with them when they emigrated to Maine in 1920. The recipe calls for peeled cucumbers which is unusual, and it doesn't call for processing in a hot water bath, but I've updated it to follow modern food safety standards.

## INGREDIENTS

- Pickling cucumbers
- Onions
- ¼ cup canning salt
- 1 quart apple cider vinegar
- 2 cups brown sugar
- 1 Tbsp dry mustard
- 1 Tbsp turmeric
- 1 Tbsp ClearJel (optional)
- Ball Pickle Crisp (optional)

## YIELD

Makes 6-8 pints

## RECIPE

1. Wash, peel, and slice cucumbers and onions. Place in a bowl and cover them with ice-cold water and salt. Let stand 12 hours or overnight.
2. Bring vinegar and sugar to a boil. Mix dry mustard, turmeric, and ClearJel. Add a little vinegar to form a paste, then add to boiling vinegar and sugar. Stir well to mix.
3. Drain and rinse cucumbers and onions under cold water. Place vegetables in the brine and boil softly for 5 minutes. Pack into prepared jars, leaving ½-inch headspace. Add brine to cover, remove air bubbles, add sterilized lids and bands to finger tight. Add 1/8 tsp Pickle Crisp to each pint jar.

4. Using a jar lifter, carefully place each jar in a hot water bath canner. Make sure the jars are not crowded and are covered with water. Add more boiling water if needed. Cover pot and return to a boil.
5. After 5 minutes, shut off the heat and remove the lid. Wait another 5 minutes, and then using a jar lifter, place each jar upright on a wire rack or towel. Allow to cool completely. Although you could eat these pickles immediately, I suggest waiting one or two weeks to allow the flavors to develop fully. Be sure to label each jar. Before storing, remove the bands. Do not stack the jars on top of each other.

# Bread and Butter Pickles

Just like Grandma used to make!

## INGREDIENTS

- 10 cups sliced, trimmed pickling cucumbers
- 4 medium onions sliced thinly
- ½ cup canning salt
- 3 cups white vinegar
- 2 cups granulated sugar
- 2 Tbsp mustard seed
- 1 tsp celery seed
- 1 tsp turmeric
- ¼ tsp Pickle Crisp per pint (optional)

## YIELD

5 pints

## RECIPE

1. Prepare pickling cucumbers making sure to trim off and discard the blossom end. Combine cucumber slices, onions, and salt in a large glass bowl. Mix. Add ice-cold water, cover, and allow to sit for 2 hours. After 2 hours, drain, rinse with cool water, and set aside.
2. Prepare hot water bath canner, jars, and lids.
3. In a large stainless-steel saucepan, combine vinegar, sugar, and spices. Bring to a boil over medium-high heat, stirring to dissolve sugar. Add cucumbers and onions and return to a boil.
4. Pack cucumbers and onions into hot jars, leaving ½-inch headspace. Using a jar funnel, ladle hot brine to cover, remove air bubbles with a rubber spatula. Add Pickle Crisp if desired.
5. Wipe rims, add lids and bands to finger tight.
6. Using a jar lifter, carefully place each jar in the boiling hot water bath. Make sure the jars are not crowded and are covered with water. Add more boiling water if needed. Cover pot and bring to a boil.
7. Return to a boil and process for 10 minutes. Remove canner from heat and remove the lid. Wait another 5 minutes, and then, using a jar lifter, place each jar upright on a wire rack or towel. Cool, label, and remove bands. Although you could eat these pickles immediately, I suggest waiting one or two weeks to allow the flavors to develop fully.

# Watermelon Rind Pickles

Rather than tossing the rinds in the compost pile, make pickles. Give this vintage recipe a try. Waste not, want not!

## INGREDIENTS

- Rind of 1 large watermelon
- 4 Tbsp canning salt
- Water
- 8 cups granulated sugar
- 4 cups white vinegar
- 8 tsp whole cloves
- 16 cinnamon sticks
- 1 tsp mustard seed
- Green or red food coloring (optional)

## YIELD

Varies

## RECIPE

1. Peel and remove all pink and green portions from the rind of 1 large watermelon. Cut rind into 1-inch cubes and soak overnight in 1 quart water mixed with 4 Tbsp canning salt.
2. Next day, drain and add to a large stainless-steel saucepan. Cover with fresh water and cook over medium heat until the rind is almost tender. Drain.
3. Make a cheesecloth spice bag with cloves, cinnamon sticks, and mustard seed. In the saucepan, add sugar, vinegar, and spice bag. Heat the syrup to boiling, then simmer for 15 minutes.
4. Prepare hot water bath canner, jars, and lids.
5. Add rinds to syrup and cook until clear and transparent. Add a few drops of food coloring (optional).
6. Using a slotted spoon, pack rinds into hot jars, leaving ½-inch headspace. Using a jar funnel, ladle hot syrup to cover, leaving ½-inch headspace. Remove air bubbles with a rubber spatula. Add more syrup if needed.
7. Wipe rims, add lids and bands to finger tight.
8. Using a jar lifter, carefully place each jar in a boiling hot water bath. Make sure the jars are not crowded and are covered with water. Add more boiling water if needed. Cover pot and return to a boil.

9. Process for 5 minutes. Remove canner from heat and remove the lid. Wait another 5 minutes, and then using a jar lifter, place each jar upright on a wire rack or towel. Cool, label, and remove bands.

# Down East Sour Pickles

Another family recipe. You can be creative with this recipe and slice, quarter, or halve the cucumbers (blossom end removed) or cut into spears. This is an old-fashioned Down East sour pickle. My grandmother poured the hot brine into the jars and added the lids and bands, but I suggest a brief hot water bath to comply with modern food safety standards.

## INGREDIENTS

- Cucumbers
- 3 cups vinegar
- 1 cup water
- ¼ cup canning salt
- ¼ cup granulated sugar
- ¼ cup dry mustard
- ¼ tsp Ball Pickle Crisp per pint (optional)

## YEILD

Makes 4 pints

## Luke's Variation

Add 1/8 tsp mustard seed to each jar.

## RECIPE

1. Prepare cucumbers as desired. Add to sterilized canning jars, leaving headspace.
2. Add vinegar, water, salt, sugar, and dry mustard to the pot and bring it to a hard boil.
3. Pour hot brine over cucumbers leaving ½-inch headspace. Add Pickle Crisp to each jar. (optional)
4. Wipe rims, add lids and bands to finger tight.
5. Add jars to a hot water bath canner. Cover. Return to a boil. Process for 5 minutes.
6. Shut off heat and remove the lid. Wait another 5 minutes, and then using a jar lifter, place each jar upright on a wire rack or towel. Cool completely. Although you could eat these pickles immediately, I suggest waiting one or two weeks to allow the flavors to develop fully. Be sure to label each jar with what it holds and the date it was canned for long-term storage. Before storing, remove the bands. Do not stack the jars on top of each other.

# Ice Water Pickle Spears

Another vintage recipe that I've adjusted slightly. Serve on a vintage pickle dish at your next dinner party!

## INGREDIENTS

- 6 lbs medium cucumbers
- 3 quarts white vinegar
- 3 cups granulated sugar
- 1 cup canning salt
- Mustard seed
- Celery stalks
- Pickling onions
- Ball Pickle Crisp (optional)

## YIELD

Use quart jars to accommodate long spears

## RECIPE

1. Remove blossom end and slice cucumbers into spears. Scrape off excess seeds.
2. Soak spears in ice water for 3 hours.
3. Add 6 small, peeled pickling onions, 2 stalks trimmed celery, and 1 tsp mustard seed to each jar.
4. Drain cucumbers and pack spears into jars.
5. Mix vinegar, sugar, and salt. Bring to a hard boil.
6. Pour brine solution into jars leaving ½-inch headspace.
7. Add 1 tsp Ball Pickle Crisp to each quart jar.
8. Wipe rims, add lids and bands to finger tight.
9. Add jars to a hot water bath canner. Cover. Return to a boil. Process for 5 minutes.
10. Shut off heat and remove the lid. Wait another 5 minutes, and then using a jar lifter, place each jar upright on a wire rack or towel. Label jars and store them in a cool, dark place.

# End of Harvest Pickled Vegetable Mix

This is a great way to make effective use of small amounts of lots of things at the end of the gardening season.

## INGREDIENTS

- 3 cups sliced zucchini
- 3 cups sliced, trimmed green or yellow beans
- 1½ cups peeled, sliced carrots
- 2 cups peeled pickling or pearl onions
- 3 green or red bell peppers, seeded and cut into thin strips
- 3 cups apple cider vinegar
- 1 cup brown sugar
- 1 cup granulated sugar
- 2 Tbsp dry mustard
- 2 Tbsp mustard seed
- 5 tsp canning salt
- 1 tsp ground cinnamon
- 1 tsp ground ginger

## YIELD

Makes about 5 pints

## RECIPE

1. Prepare hot water bath canner, jars, and lids.
2. In a large glass bowl, combine all vegetables. Mix well and set aside.
3. In a large stainless-steel saucepan, combine vinegar, sugars, and all spices. Bring to a boil over medium-high heat, stirring to dissolve sugar. Add vegetable mix and return to a boil. Reduce heat and boil gently for 15 minutes.
4. Using a slotted spoon and a jar funnel, pack hot vegetables into hot jars, leaving ½-inch headspace. Add pickling brine to cover, remove air bubbles using a rubber spatula. Add lids and bands to finger tight.
5. Using a jar lifter, carefully place each jar in the boiling hot water bath. Make sure the jars are not crowded and are covered with water. Add more boiling water if needed. Cover pot and bring to a boil. Process pints for 15 minutes.
6. Shut off heat and remove the lid. Wait another 5 minutes, and then using a jar lifter, place each jar upright on a wire rack or towel. When cool, remove bands, label, and store in a cool, dark place.

# Pickled Red Cabbage

Even people who claim they hate cabbage will love this spicy pickled treat!

## INGREDIENTS

- 12 lbs red cabbage
- ½ cup canning salt
- ¼ cup whole cloves
- ¼ cup whole allspice
- ¼ cup whole black peppercorns
- ¼ cup celery seed
- 2 cinnamon sticks
- 8 cups red wine vinegar
- 1 cup brown sugar
- ½ cup mustard seed
- ¼ cup ground nutmeg

## YIELD

Makes about 9 pints

## Luke's Variation

Use green cabbage or a combination of both.

## RECIPE

1. Core red cabbage and shred using a very sharp knife or mandoline. Working in batches, place in a colander and rinse under cold water. Transfer to a baking sheet and drain between layers of paper towels for 5-6 hours.
2. Prepare hot water bath canner, jars, and lids.
3. Make a spice bag with cheesecloth. Tie cloves, allspice, peppercorns, celery seed, and cinnamon sticks broken into pieces in cheesecloth.
4. Bring vinegar, brown sugar, mustard seed, nutmeg, and spice bag to a boil over medium-high heat in a large stainless-steel saucepan. Reduce heat and boil gently for 5-10 minutes. Discard spice bag.
5. Pack the cabbage into hot jars, leaving ½-inch headspace. Using a jar funnel, pour the hot pickling liquid over cabbage, leaving ½ inch headspace. Use a rubber spatula to remove air bubbles. Add more liquid if necessary.
6. Wipe rims with a paper towel moistened with vinegar. Add lids and bands to finger tight.
7. Add jars to a hot water bath canner. Cover. Return to a boil. Process for 20 minutes.
8. Shut off heat and remove the lid. Wait another 5 minutes, and then using a jar lifter, place each jar upright on a wire rack or towel. Allow to cool completely. Remove bands, label, and store in a cool, dark place.

# Dilly Beans

Use a combination of green, yellow, and purple beans for a spectacular effect!

## INGREDIENTS

- 3 Tbsp canning salt
- 3 cups white vinegar
- 3 cups water
- 4-5 lbs beans
- 2-3 sweet red bell peppers
- Peppercorns
- Fresh dill
- Garlic cloves

## YIELD

Makes about 6 pints

## RECIPE

1. Prepare hot water bath canner, jars, and lids.
2. In a large stainless-steel saucepan, combine salt, vinegar, and water. Bring to a boil over medium-high heat. Add beans cut into jar-sized pieces and thinly sliced red pepper strips. Return to a boil. Remove from heat.
3. Place 3-5 peppercorns, a generous sprig of dill, or ½ tsp of dill seed if fresh dill is unavailable, and 1 peeled garlic clove to each jar. Add beans and pepper strips to each jar, leaving ½-inch headspace. Use a rubber spatula to remove air bubbles. Add more liquid if necessary.

4. Wipe rims with a paper towel moistened with vinegar. Add lids and bands to finger tight.
5. Add jars to boiling water bath. Cover. Return to a boil. Process for 10 minutes.
6. Shut off heat and remove the lid. Wait another 5 minutes, and then using a jar lifter, place each jar upright on a wire rack or towel. Allow to cool completely. Remove bands, label, and store in a cool, dark place.

# Dilly Carrots

Add to salads, sandwiches, or relish trays. Try using rainbow carrots!

## INGREDIENTS

- 6 cups white vinegar
- 2 cups water
- ½ cup canning salt
- Garlic cloves
- Fresh dill or dill seed
- 3½ tsp red pepper flakes (optional)
- 5 lbs carrots
- Peppercorns

## YIELD

Makes about 7 pints

## RECIPE

1. Prepare hot water bath canner, jars, and lids.
2. Peel carrots and remove ends. Using a mandoline or sharp knife, cut carrots into sticks.
3. In a large stainless-steel saucepan, combine salt, vinegar, and water. Bring to a boil over medium-high heat, stirring to dissolve the salt.
4. Place 1 garlic clove, 3-5 peppercorns, a generous sprig of dill, or ½ tsp of dill seed if fresh dill is unavailable, and ½ tsp red pepper flakes to each jar. Pack carrots into jars, leaving ½-inch headspace. Ladle hot pickling brine over carrots leaving ½-inch headspace. Use a rubber spatula to remove air bubbles. Add more brine if necessary.
5. Wipe rims with a paper towel moistened with vinegar. Add lids and bands to finger tight.
6. Add jars to boiling water bath. Cover. Return to a boil. Process for 10 minutes.
7. Shut off heat and remove the lid. Wait another 5 minutes, and then using a jar lifter, place each jar upright on a towel or wire rack. Allow to cool completely. Remove bands, label, and store in a cool, dark place.

# Do Chua (Vietnamese Carrot and Daikon Radish Pickles)

Try these Asian sweet pickles on a sandwich once, and the jar will be empty before you know it!

## INGREDIENTS

- 3 cups white vinegar
- 3 cups water
- 1½ cups granulated sugar
- 2 tsp grated ginger root
- 2 lbs carrots
- 2 lbs daikon radish
- 6 whole star anise (optional)

## YIELD

Makes about 6 pints

## RECIPE

1. Prepare hot water bath canner, jars, and lids.
2. Peel carrots and remove ends. Peel daikon. Using a mandoline or an extremely sharp knife, julienne the carrots and radishes into very thin strips.
3. In a large stainless-steel saucepan, combine sugar, vinegar, water, and ginger root. Bring to a boil over medium-high heat, stirring to dissolve sugar. Add carrot and daikon and stir for 1 minute. Remove from heat.
4. Add 1 star anise (if using) to each jar. Pack hot vegetables into hot jars, leaving ½-inch headspace. Ladle hot pickling liquid into each jar to cover vegetables leaving ½-inch headspace. Use a rubber spatula to remove air bubbles. Add more liquid if necessary.
5. Wipe rims with a paper towel moistened with vinegar. Add lids and bands to finger tight.
6. Add jars to boiling water bath. Cover. Return to a boil. Process for 10 minutes.
7. Shut off heat and remove the lid. Wait another 5 minutes and then, using a jar lifter, place each jar upright on a wire rack or towel. Allow to cool completely. Remove bands, label, and store in a cool, dark place.

## Banh Mi (Vietnamese Sandwich) Recipe

Banh Mi is a traditional Vietnamese sandwich sold by street vendors made on a crusty bread roll, or French bread, smeared with mayo. Add your choice of grilled meat and a heap of Do Chua. Top with green onion, coriander/cilantro, and sliced jalapeno peppers. Your new favorite sandwich!

# Sweet Pickled Beets

Besides being rich in vitamins and minerals, pickled beets are delicious and heart-healthy!

## INGREDIENTS

- 10 whole cloves
- 2 cinnamon sticks
- 2½ cups white vinegar
- 1 cup water
- 1 cup granulated sugar
- 10 cups prepared beets

## YIELD

Makes about 6 pints

## RECIPE

1. To prepare beets, leave the roots and two inches stem intact. Scrub thoroughly to remove dirt. Place in a saucepan and bring to boil. Reduce heat and cook until tender. Remove beets and run under cold water. Slip off the skins, remove stem and taproot. Leave small beets whole or slice or quarter larger beets.
2. Prepare hot water bath canner, jars, and lids.
3. Make a spice bag with cheesecloth. Tie cloves and cinnamon sticks broken into pieces in cheesecloth.
4. In a large stainless-steel saucepan, bring vinegar, sugar, water, and spice bag to a boil over medium-high heat, stirring to dissolve sugar. Reduce heat and boil gently for 15 minutes. Discard spice bag.
5. Using a slotted spoon and jar funnel, add beets to hot jars, leaving ½-inch headspace. Pour hot pickling liquid over beets leaving ½-inch headspace. Use a rubber spatula to remove air bubbles. Add more liquid if necessary.
6. Wipe rims with a paper towel moistened with vinegar. Add lids and bands to finger tight.
7. Add jars to boiling water bath. Cover. Return to a boil. Process for 30 minutes.

8. Shut off heat and remove the lid. Wait another 5 minutes, and then, using a jar lifter, place each jar upright on a wire rack or towel on the counter. Allow to cool completely. Remove bands, label, and store in a cool, dark place.

**Sweet Pickled Beets and Onions:** Add 3 cups peeled and thinly sliced Vidalia onions to the pickling liquid and cook as directed in Step 4. Use only 8 cups of prepared beets.

# Traditional Fermented Sauerkraut

Fermented foods, like this sauerkraut, are rich in probiotic bacteria. Consumption of fermented foods adds beneficial bacteria and enzymes to your digestive system and enhances the immune system.

## INGREDIENTS

- 5 lbs cabbage
- 3½ Tbsp canning salt

## YIELD

Makes about 5 pints

## Note

You'll need a large crock to ferment the kraut. An extra-large crockpot would suffice.

## RECIPE

1. Prepare cabbage by removing the outer leaves. Rinse well under cool water. Quarter the heads and shred cabbage finely.
2. Place 5 pounds of cabbage and canning salt into a large pan and mix with clean hands. Pack salted cabbage into the crock pressing down with a potato masher until the crock is full.
3. Cover with a plate, a weight, and a cloth. Every day, remove the scum as it forms and cover with a clean cloth. Fermentation will be complete in 10-12 days.
4. Once the kraut is thoroughly cured, I suggest taste-testing it. When satisfied with the flavor, pack it into hot, clean jars. Add kraut juice to cover, leaving ½-inch headspace. If you run out of liquid, dissolve 2 Tbsp canning salt in 1 quart water and use that to top off jars.
5. Wipe rims with a paper towel moistened with vinegar. Add lids and bands to finger tight.
6. Process pints in hot water bath canner for 20 minutes.
7. Remove from heat. Remove lid, wait 5 minutes, then remove jars from canner. Cool, remove bands, label, and store jars.

# State Fair Pickled Three-Bean Salad

A traditional church picnic and family reunion favorite for generations. Try this award-winning recipe!

## INGREDIENTS

- 4½ cups green beans
- 4½ cups yellow beans
- 1 lb lima beans (fresh or frozen)
- 2 cups celery
- 2 cups sliced onions
- 1 large sweet red bell pepper
- Boiling water
- 2½ cups granulated sugar
- 1 Tbsp mustard seed
- 1 tsp celery seed
- 4 tsp canning salt
- 3 cups white vinegar
- 1¼ cups water

## YIELD

Makes about 5-6 pints

## RECIPE

1. Prepare hot water bath canner, jars, and lids.
2. Trim beans to 1-1½-inch slices. Slice celery into ½-inch slices. Shell lima beans if fresh or defrost if frozen. Peel and thinly slice onions. Core and dice red pepper.
3. Add all vegetables to a large stainless-steel saucepan. Add boiling water to cover. Return to a boil over medium-high heat. Reduce heat and boil gently for 5 minutes to heat vegetables.
4. Meanwhile, in a separate stainless-steel saucepan, prepare your pickling brine. Combine sugar, mustard seed, celery seed, salt, vinegar, and water. Bring to a boil over medium-high heat, stirring to dissolve sugar. Reduce heat and boil gently for 5 minutes.
5. Drain hot vegetables and pack into hot jars, leaving ½-inch headspace. Pour hot pickling liquid over vegetables leaving ½-inch headspace. Use a rubber spatula to remove air bubbles. Add more liquid if necessary.
6. Wipe rims with a paper towel moistened with vinegar. Add lids and bands to finger tight.
7. Add jars to boiling water bath. Cover. Return to a boil. Process pints for 15 minutes.

8. Shut off heat and remove the lid. Wait another 5 minutes and then, using a jar lifter, place each jar upright on a wire rack or towel on the counter. Allow to cool completely. Remove bands, label, and store in a cool, dark place.

# No-Cook Pickled Hot Pepper Mix

This vintage recipe doesn't call for processing in a hot water bath. Assuming the lids "ping" you should be fine. To be extra-safe, store in refrigerator or process for 5 minutes in a hot water bath.

## INGREDIENTS

- Any combination of hot peppers
- Canning salt
- Water
- White vinegar
- Fresh dill or dill seed
- Grape or oak leaf*
- Garlic clove

## YIELD

Varies

## Note

Quart jars are an excellent choice to accommodate long banana or Hungarian peppers.

## RECIPE

**Day One**

1. Wash peppers.
2. Cut 2 small slits in each pepper. Place the peppers in a large ceramic bowl or stainless-steel pot.
3. Add 2 quarts of cool water and 1 cup canning salt to the bowl. Submerge peppers using a large plate with a weight on the top to keep peppers submerged in the brine. You can use a Mason jar filled with water as the weight. Set in a cool place overnight.

**Day Two**

1. Prepare jars and lids.
2. Drain well and pack peppers into hot quart jars.
3. Mix 2 quarts water, ½ cup canning salt, ½ cup vinegar, 1 garlic clove, 1 grape or oak leaf, and a bunch of fresh dill or 1 tsp of dill seed in a large stainless-steel saucepan. Bring to a rapid boil.
4. Pour boiling brine over peppers filling and sealing one jar at a time, leaving ½-inch headspace. Do not remove bands. Label and store.

**Optional**

5. Using a jar lifter, carefully place each jar in a hot water bath canner. Make sure the jars are not crowded and are covered with water. Add more boiling water if needed. Cover pot and return to a boil. Process for 5 minutes.
6. Shut off heat and remove the lid. Wait another 5 minutes, and then, using a jar lifter, place each jar upright on a towel or wire rack. When cool, remove bands, label, and store in a cool, dark place.

*Black tea leaves, oak leaves, grape leaves, or horseradish leaves all add tannins to the pickle brine resulting in crisper pickles. If you don't have them available, use Ball Pickle Crisp. Use ¾ tsp per pint or 1½ tsp per quart.

# Pickled Hot Peppers

This modern recipe calls for processing in a hot water bath. They're great on sandwiches, pizza, anytime you need a kick. You can focus on one type of pepper per jar, jalapeno, for instance, or mix it up for a variety of heat!

## INGREDIENTS

- 2 quarts hot peppers, any variety
- 2 cups white vinegar
- 2 cups water
- Canning salt

## YIELD

4 pints

## Note

If you like a lot of heat, leave most or all the seeds intact.

## RECIPE

1. Prepare hot water bath canner, jars, and lids.
2. Rinse peppers under cool water. Remove stem, cores, and some or all the seeds. Slice into ½-inch rings. Or, if you prefer, leave small peppers whole and cut 2 small slits on each side so they don't explode during the canning process.
3. Mix the vinegar and water in a large stainless-steel saucepan. Bring to a boil.
4. Pour boiling brine over peppers leaving ½-inch headspace. Add ½ tsp canning salt to each jar. Remove air bubbles, wipe rims, add lids and bands to finger tight.
5. Using a jar lifter, carefully place each jar in the boiling hot water bath. Make sure the jars are not crowded and are covered with water. Add more boiling water if needed. Cover pot and return to a boil. Process for 5 minutes.
6. Shut off heat and remove the lid. Wait another 5 minutes, and then using a jar lifter, place each jar upright on a wire rack or towel. When cool, remove bands, label, and store in a cool, dark place.

*Black tea leaves, oak leaves, grape leaves, or horseradish leaves all add tannins to the pickle brine resulting in crisper peppers. Discard leaves before adding pickling brine to jars. Or, if you don't have them available, use Ball Pickle Crisp. Use ¾ tsp per pint or 1½ tsp per quart. Add to jars immediately before sealing.

# 14-Day Sweet Pickles

This vintage recipe takes 2 weeks to prepare, so write the steps down on a calendar. It doesn't call for processing in a hot water bath but use your judgment. Adjust the recipe to suit your desired yield.

## INGREDIENTS

- 2 gallons of cucumbers
- 2 cups canning salt
- Water
- 1 Tbsp powdered alum
- 5 pints vinegar
- 6 cups granulated sugar
- 5 tsp celery seed
- 2-3 cinnamon sticks

## YIELD

Varies

## RECIPE

**Day 1:** Place cucumbers with blossom end trimmed and sliced lengthwise into a clean crock or large crockpot. Dissolve 2 cups of canning salt in 1 gallon of boiling water and pour over cucumbers. Weigh down cucumbers, so they stay submerged with a plate. Cover and let stand undisturbed for 1 week in a cool place.

**Day 8:** Drain water and replace with 1 gallon of boiling water, ensuring cucumbers are submerged. Cover and let stand for 24 hours.

**Day 9:** Drain water and replace with 1 gallon of boiling water mixed with 1 Tbsp of powdered alum. Cover and let stand for 24 hours.

**Day 10:** Drain again and replace with 1 gallon of boiling water. Let stand for 24 hours, then drain.

**Day 11:** In a large stainless-steel saucepan, combine 5 pints of vinegar, 6 cups of granulated sugar, celery seed, and cinnamon stick broken into pieces. Bring to a boil and pour this mixture over the cucumbers. Cover and let stand 24 hours.

**Day 12:** Drain and reserve liquid. Add 1 cup sugar to the reserved liquid. Heat to boiling and repour over pickles. Cover and let stand for 24 hours.

**Day 13:** Drain and reserve liquid. Add 1 cup sugar to the reserved liquid. Heat to boiling and repour over pickles. Cover and let stand for 24 hours.

**Day 14:** Drain and reserve liquid. Add 1 cup sugar to the reserved liquid. Reheat to boiling. Pack pickles in sterilized, hot jars. Pour hot syrup over pickles. Wipe rims with a paper towel moistened with vinegar. Add lids, bands, and seal. Allow to cool on a wire rack. If the lids "ping" you have a successful seal.

# RELISHES & SALSA

I only included one salsa recipe because it's a fairly new addition to North American diets. Relishes have been around forever and have a variety of uses besides hot dogs and burgers. Relishes may have originated to utilize an abundance of homegrown fruits and vegetables. Relish will take about two weeks to develop maximum flavor.

# Taste of Summer Vegetable Salsa

Salsa, long a part of Mexican cuisine, became popular in the United States in Mexican restaurants in the 1980s. So, your grandmother never even heard of it. But I've included it here because of its modern popularity. Plus, it's a great way to use garden tomatoes, onions, peppers, and herbs.

## INGREDIENTS

- 7 cups peeled, cored, chopped tomatoes
- 2 cups chopped onion
- 1 cup chopped green bell pepper
- 8 seeded and finely chopped jalapeno or other hot peppers (or less to taste)
- 3 garlic cloves minced
- 1 5.5oz can tomato paste
- ¾ cup white vinegar
- ½ cup chopped cilantro
- ½ tsp ground cumin
- Canning salt and freshly ground black pepper to taste

## YIELD

4 pints

## RECIPE

1. Add all ingredients to a large stainless-steel saucepan. Bring to a boil over medium-high heat, stirring often. Reduce heat to medium and boil gently for about 30 minutes until the mixture thickens to desired consistency. The more mixture evaporates, the thicker your salsa will be.
2. Meanwhile, prepare a hot water bath canner, jars, and lids.
3. Using a jar funnel, pour hot salsa into jars leaving ½-inch headspace. Wipe rims with a paper towel moistened with vinegar. Add lids and bands to finger tight.
4. Using a jar lifter, carefully place each jar in the boiling hot water bath. Make sure the jars are not crowded and are covered with water. Add more boiling water if needed. Cover pot and return to a boil. Process both 8-ounce and pint jars for 20 minutes. Remove from heat, remove the cover, and remove jars after 5 minutes. Cool on a wire rack, label, and store.

## TIPS

You can use any variety of hot pepper. If you want it milder, reduce the number of hot peppers and remove the seeds and veins before chopping. Or for a very mild salsa, eliminate the hot peppers. But, if you like it fiery, include the seeds!

# Sweet Relish

Another hand-me-down family recipe from my grandmother. It helps if you have a food grinder. You can often find these at second-hand shops, flea markets, and yard sales. Or use a food processor with a metal blade. Great on hot dogs, burgers, when making deviled eggs, and more!

## INGREDIENTS

- 7 cucumbers peeled and cored
- 3 green tomatoes
- 1 green bell pepper cored and seeded
- 1 sweet red bell pepper cored and seeded
- 3 stalks celery
- 3 onions
- ½ head large cabbage
- 3 cups white vinegar
- 1 cup water
- 1 lb brown sugar
- 1 tsp ground clove
- 1 tsp cinnamon
- 2 tsp turmeric
- ½ tsp mustard seed
- 1 Tbsp canning salt

## YIELD

8 8oz jars (My grandmother used repurposed mustard jars)

## RECIPE

1. Grind all the vegetables. Mix in a large bowl. Sprinkle with 1 Tbsp canning salt. Cover and let stand for 2 hours. Drain liquid and set aside.
2. Bring vinegar, water, and spices to a boil in a large stainless-steel pot. Add all ground vegetables. Return to a boil. Reduce heat and simmer uncovered for 1 hour.
3. Pack into hot jars, leaving ½-inch headspace. Wipe rims with a paper towel moistened with vinegar. Add lids and bands to finger tight.
4. Using a jar lifter, carefully place each jar in a hot water bath canner. Make sure the jars are not crowded and are covered with water. Add more boiling water if needed. Cover pot and return to a boil. Process both 8oz and pint jars for 10 minutes. Remove from heat, remove the cover, and remove jars after 5 minutes. Cool, label, and store.

# Dill Relish

This is a great way to use those end-of-season cucumbers and the dill seed you harvested and saved from earlier in the season. Kids love this traditional family favorite!

## INGREDIENTS

- 8 lbs pickling cucumbers
- ½ cup canning salt
- 2 tsp ground turmeric
- 4 cups cold water
- 2½ cups finely chopped onions
- 1/3 cup granulated sugar
- 2 Tbsp dill seed
- 4 cups white vinegar

## YIELD

7 pints

## RECIPE

1. In a food processor or using a food grinder, finely chop cucumbers working in small batches. Transfer to a large bowl.
2. Sprinkle canning salt and turmeric over cucumbers. Mix to blend. Add cold water, cover the bowl, and let stand in a cool place for 2-3 hours.
3. Pour cucumbers into a large colander placed over sink and drain. Rinse with cool water and drain again. Squeeze out excess moisture using your clean hands.
4. Prepare hot water bath canner, jars, and lids.
5. Add drained cucumbers, onions, sugar, dill seed, and vinegar to a large stainless-steel pot. Bring to a boil over medium-high heat, stirring to prevent scorching. Reduce heat and boil gently, uncovered, for 10-15 minutes until relish begins to thicken.
6. Using a jar funnel, ladle hot relish into hot jars, leaving ½-inch headspace. Wipe rims with a paper towel moistened with vinegar, add lids, and bands to finger tight.
7. Using a jar lifter, carefully place each jar in a boiling hot water bath. Make sure the jars are not crowded and are covered with water. Add more boiling water if needed. Cover pot and return to a boil. Process both 8oz and pint jars for 15 minutes. Remove from heat, remove the cover, and remove jars after 5 minutes. Cool, label, and store.

# Victory Garden Red Pepper Relish

A pretty and delicious alternative to green relishes, this family favorite is circa WWII.

## INGREDIENTS

- 24 sweet red bell peppers
- 7 medium onions (I prefer Vidalia when in season)
- 2 Tbsp mustard seed
- 2 Tbsp canning salt
- 3 cups white vinegar
- 3 cups granulated sugar

## YIELD

Use 4oz, 8oz, or pint jars

## Note

During WWII, this relish was prepared and packed hot into hot jars. Home canners added the lids and bands, but they did not use a hot water bath. I suggest processing it to meet modern-day food safety standards.

## RECIPE

1. In a food processor or using a food grinder, grind peppers and onions. Save the juice.
2. Combine the ground vegetables, juice, and all other ingredients in a large stainless-steel saucepan. Bring to a boil over medium-high heat, stirring to prevent scorching. Reduce heat and boil gently, uncovered, for 30 minutes, stirring often, until the relish begins to thicken.
3. Prepare hot water bath canner, jars, and lids.
4. Using a jar funnel, ladle hot relish into hot jars, leaving ½-inch headspace. Wipe rims with a paper towel moistened with vinegar, add lids, and bands to finger tight.
5. Using a jar lifter, carefully place each jar in the boiling hot water bath. Make sure the jars are not crowded and are covered with water. Add more boiling water if needed. Cover pot and return to a boil. Process 4oz, 8oz, and pint jars for 10 minutes. Remove from heat, remove the cover, and remove jars after 5 minutes. Cool, label, and store

# County Fair Corn Relish

Use as a condiment for burgers and hot dogs or as a flavorful side dish for Tex-Mex or Mexican cuisine. Prepare this when sweet corn is in season.

## INGREDIENTS

- 4 cups white vinegar
- 1¼ cups granulated sugar
- 2 Tbsp canning salt
- 8 cups corn kernels*
- 2 cups diced red bell pepper
- 2 cups diced green bell pepper
- 2 cups diced celery
- 1 cup finely chopped onion
- 2 Tbsp dry mustard
- 2 tsp celery seed
- 2 tsp ground turmeric
- ¼ cup water
- 2 Tbsp ClearJel

## YIELD

12 8oz jars or 6 pints

## RECIPE

1. Prepare hot water bath canner, jars, and lids.
2. In a large stainless-steel saucepan, combine vinegar, sugar, and salt. Bring to a boil over medium-high heat, stirring to dissolve sugar. Gradually add all vegetables and stir constantly to prevent scorching. Stir in seasonings while keeping a boil. In a small bowl, mix water and ClearJel with a fork. Stir into the boiling mixture. Reduce heat and boil gently for 5-10 minutes until relish begins to thicken.
3. Using a jar funnel, ladle hot relish into hot jars, leaving ½-inch headspace. Wipe rims with a paper towel moistened with vinegar, add lids, and bands to finger tight.
4. Using a jar lifter, carefully place each jar in a boiling hot water bath. Make sure the jars are not crowded and are covered with water. Add more boiling water if needed. Cover pot and return to a boil. Process both 8oz and pint jars for 15 minutes. Remove from heat, remove the cover, and remove jars after 5 minutes. Cool, label, and store.

*When using fresh corn, blanch ears for 5 minutes in boiling water before removing kernels.

# Green Tomato Relish

Another family favorite. This is an excellent recipe for end-of-the-season tomatoes that will not have time to ripen before the first frost.

## INGREDIENTS

- 6 cups unpeeled, cored, chopped green tomatoes
- 2 onions finely chopped
- 2 green bell peppers finely chopped
- 1 red bell pepper finely chopped
- ¼ cup canning salt
- 1 tsp ground clove
- 1 tsp celery seed
- 1 cinnamon stick
- 2 cups white vinegar
- 1½ cups brown sugar
- 1 garlic clove finely chopped
- 1 Tbsp dry mustard
- ½ tsp canning salt
- ½ tsp ground ginger

## YIELD

6 8oz jars

## RECIPE

1. Add prepared tomatoes, onions, peppers, and canning salt to a large glass or stainless-steel bowl. Cover and let stand in a cool place for 12 hours. Drain in a colander. Rinse with cool water, drain, and squeeze out excess moisture with clean hands.
2. Create a spice bag by tying cloves, celery seed, and cinnamon stick (broken in half) in a square of cheesecloth. Set aside.
3. In a large stainless-steel saucepan, mix vinegar, brown sugar, garlic, mustard, remaining salt, ginger, and spice bag. Bring to a boil over medium-high heat, stirring to dissolve sugar and prevent scorching. Add drained tomatoes and return to a boil. Reduce heat and boil gently, stirring often, for about 1 hour. Discard spice bag.
4. Meanwhile, prepare a hot water bath canner, jars, and lids.
5. Using a jar funnel, pour or ladle hot relish into hot jars, leaving ½-inch headspace. Wipe rims with a paper towel moistened with vinegar. Add lids and bands to finger tight.
6. Using a jar lifter, carefully place each jar in the boiling hot water bath. Make sure the jars are not crowded and are covered with water. Add more boiling water if needed. Cover pot and return to a boil. Process for 10 minutes. Remove from heat, remove the cover, and remove jars after 5 minutes. Cool, label, and store.

# VINEGARS

Great as a basis for salad dressings, flavored vinegars are easy to make and are a great gift!

# Legendary 4 Thieves Vinegar Tonic

Legend has it that during the 18th-century plague epidemic in Europe, a band of thieves robbed the homes and graves of those who were sick and dying of the disease but never fell ill themselves. Their secret? They doused cloth face coverings in a tonic they had created and washed their hands with it after robbing the graves. When finally captured, they shared their secret recipe. This vinegar acts as an antiseptic and to disinfect, repel insects, and boost the immune system when taken as a tonic. You can make it using fresh herbs from your garden and mix and match to suit your needs and tastes.

## INGREDIENTS

- Garlic cloves
- Whole cloves
- Cinnamon sticks
- Rosemary
- Thyme
- Oregano
- Sage
- Lavender (optional)
- 32oz organic apple cider vinegar
- Black peppercorns (optional)
- Ginger root (optional)
- Mason jars or decorative bottles with corks or stoppers

## YIELD

4 pints

## RECIPE

1. Place garlic, cloves, and herbs (fresh or dried) in each jar.
2. Add cinnamon sticks, peppercorns, and grated ginger root to organic apple cider vinegar in a large stainless-steel saucepan. Bring to a gentle boil, reduce heat and simmer for 5-10 minutes. Strain liquid.
3. Pour hot liquid over herbs in jars. Add lids or corks and place in a sunny windowsill and steep for 2-4 weeks.

**Luke's Modern Uses**

Mix with olive oil to make salad dressing.

Use in a spray bottle for cleaning kitchen/bathroom counters.

Take 1 Tbsp a day as a tonic.

Use on blemishes, cuts, fungal infections.

Apply with a cotton ball to lighten age spots.

Apply to skin to soothe sunburn.

*4 Thieves Vinegar*

# Raspberry Vinegar

Mix with balsamic vinegar for a refreshing salad dressing.

## INGREDIENTS

- 4 cups fresh or frozen raspberries
- 5 cups white wine vinegar

## YIELD

6 8oz jars

## RECIPE

1. Thaw raspberries if frozen. Add thawed or fresh raspberries to a large glass bowl. Add 1 cup of vinegar. Using a potato masher, crush raspberries but do not liquefy. Add the rest of the vinegar, stir, cover, and store in a cool, dark place for 2-4 weeks. Stir every few days. Taste weekly until the desired flavor is achieved.
2. Prepare hot water bath canner, jars, and lids.
3. Using a damp jelly bag or several layers of moistened cheesecloth, drain vinegar and solids over a large stainless-steel saucepan. Do not squeeze. Discard residue. Heat vinegar over medium heat until it is almost boiling.
4. Ladle hot vinegar into hot jars using a jar funnel, leaving ¼-inch headspace. Wipe rims, add lids and bands to finger tight.
5. Using a jar lifter, place jars in a boiling hot water bath, making sure they are covered with water. Cover canner, return to a boil, and process for 10 minutes.
6. Remove from heat, remove the cover, and remove jars after 5 minutes. Cool on a wire rack or kitchen towel. Remove bands, label, and store.

# Tarragon Vinegar

Try making this classic flavored vinegar.

## INGREDIENTS

- 2 cups white or red wine vinegar
- Fresh tarragon
- Black peppercorns

## YIELD

2 8oz jars

## Note

Add a handmade label and pretty ribbon if giving as a gift!

## RECIPE

1. In a medium stainless-steel saucepan, heat vinegar to just boiling.
2. Place sprigs of fresh tarragon and peppercorns in a sterilized jar.
3. Pour hot vinegar into a jar. Seal with a cork or non-metallic lid. Let steep for 1-2 weeks before using.

# Blueberry and Basil Vinegar

Use this flavored vinegar as the basis for a delicious salad dressing.

## INGREDIENTS

- 4 cups blueberries
- 4 cups white wine vinegar
- 1 cup fresh basil leaves
- Zest from 1 lemon

## YIELD

5 pints

## RECIPE

1. In a large glass bowl, add blueberries and 1 cup of vinegar. Lightly mash using a potato masher. Crush the basil leaves using a mortar and pestle or wooden spoon and add to the mixture. Add remaining vinegar and lemon zest. Stir, cover, and store in a cool, dark place for 3-4 weeks stirring every few days. Sample weekly until desired taste is achieved.
2. Prepare hot water bath canner, jars, and lids.
3. In a medium stainless-steel saucepan, heat vinegar to just boiling. Add a few whole, fresh blueberries to each jar.
4. Using a jar funnel, ladle hot vinegar into hot jars, leaving ¼-inch headspace. Wipe rims with a paper towel moistened with vinegar. Add lids and bands to finger tight.
5. Using a jar lifter, carefully place each jar in the boiling hot water bath. Make sure the jars are not crowded and are covered with water. Add more boiling water if needed. Cover pot and return to a boil. Process for 10 minutes. Remove from heat, remove the cover, and remove jars after 5 minutes. Cool, label, and store.

# MEAT, POULTRY & FISH

For a desirable finished product, make sure to start with high quality, lean, meat, poultry, or fish.

# Canned Chicken

This is one of the easiest recipes ever! Canned chicken is so versatile. You can use it straight out of the jar to make a chicken salad sandwich, toss some on a salad or use it in a soup or casserole. Use it in any recipe that calls for pre-cooked chicken. All you need is chicken, jars, and a few spices! It's that easy and so delicious! I recommend buying boneless, skinless chicken breasts when they're on sale, and you'll always have a supply of protein on hand. Best part? No refrigeration is necessary!

## INGREDIENTS

- Boneless, skinless chicken breasts or thighs
- Canning salt
- Freshly ground black pepper

## YIELD

Varies

## Chicken Bone-in

Canning bone-in chicken may result in more flavor. Use thighs or drumsticks that fit the jars. Cut off excess fat, leave most of the skin intact. Fill jars and follow all other steps. Reduce the processing time for the bone-in chicken to 65 minutes per pint and 75 minutes per quart at 10 pounds pressure adjusting for altitude.

## RECIPE

1. Prepare jars, lids, and pressure canner.
2. Cut up chicken into chunks.
3. Pack raw chicken into hot jars, leaving 1-inch headspace.
4. Add ½ tsp per pint or 1 tsp per quart (optional).
5. Add freshly ground pepper (optional).
6. Wipe rims, add lids and bands to finger tight. Do not add water. The chicken will make its own broth.
7. Place jars on rack in canner. Attach and secure canner lid. Heat until canner starts hissing. Allow the steam to escape the vent for 5-10 minutes, add gauge and begin timing after the first jiggle. Process pints for 75 minutes and quarts for 90 minutes at 10 pounds pressure adjusting for altitude.

**Luke's Variations**

Substitute boneless, skinless turkey breasts or thighs for chicken.
Add 1/8 tsp dried poultry seasoning to each jar.
Add a peeled garlic clove or a few onion slices to each jar.

*Canned Chicken*

# Italian Meatballs in Sauce

Just boil some pasta and all the prep work is done! You can use homemade sauce or store-bought. Your choice.

## INGREDIENTS

- Ground beef, pork, veal, turkey, or a combination to your liking
- Dried Italian breadcrumbs
- Dried Italian seasonings
- Canning salt
- Freshly ground black pepper
- Red pepper flakes (optional)
- Homemade or store-bought marinara sauce

## YIELD

Varies

## Luke's Variations

Substitute tomato juice for the marinara sauce.

Substitute beef bone broth for the marinara sauce.

## RECIPE

1. Prepare jars, lids, and pressure canner.
2. Make your favorite meatball recipe. Add breadcrumbs, dried herbs, and seasonings to ground meat. Form into 1½-inch meatballs.
3. In a skillet over medium heat, brown meatballs on all sides. Drain fat.
4. Add meatballs to jar. Do not pack. Leave 1-inch headspace.
5. Using a jar funnel, pour sauce over meatballs leaving 1-inch headspace.
6. Using a rubber spatula, remove air bubbles. Add more sauce if necessary.
7. Wipe rims with a paper towel moistened with vinegar. Add lids and bands to finger tight.
8. Carefully place jars on rack in canner. Attach and secure canner lid. Heat until canner starts hissing. Allow the steam to escape the vent for 5-10 minutes, add gauge and begin timing after the first jiggle. Process pints for 75 minutes and quarts for 90 minutes at 10 pounds pressure. Adjust timing for higher altitudes.
9. Remove canner from heat. Allow pressure to decrease naturally.
10. Remove lid. Remove jars from the canner after 5 minutes. Cool on a wire rack or kitchen towel. Remove bands, label jars, and store them in a cool, dark place.

# Chicken a la King

This vintage recipe is delicious served over egg noodles, biscuits, toast, or with a heap of mashed potatoes!

## INGREDIENTS

- 1 5-pound chicken
- 4 Tbsp ClearJel
- 1 Tbsp canning salt
- 1 quart chicken broth or homemade stock
- 1 large can sliced mushrooms
- 1 chopped green bell pepper
- 2 Tbsp pimientos or 1 chopped red bell pepper
- Freshly ground black pepper

## YIELD

5 pints

## Luke's Variations

Substitute turkey for chicken.

Substitute 1 cup fresh green peas for green pepper. Use fresh mushrooms instead of canned mushrooms.

## RECIPE

1. Prepare jars, lids, and pressure canner.
2. Cut whole chicken into pieces. Add to large stainless-steel pot. Add water to cover and bring to boil. Reduce heat, cover, and simmer for 1 hour.
3. Remove meat from bones. Discard skin. Cut meat into small pieces.
4. Dissolve ClearJel and salt in a little of the cold broth. Whisk until smooth. Add to the broth or stock and heat over medium heat, stirring constantly until smooth. The sauce will begin to thicken.
5. Add sliced mushrooms, peppers, pimientos, black pepper, and chicken. Heat to boiling, stirring constantly.
6. Using a jar funnel, pour the mixture into hot jars, leaving 1-inch headspace.
7. Using a rubber spatula, remove air bubbles. Add more sauce if necessary, leaving 1-inch headspace.
8. Wipe rims with a paper towel moistened with vinegar. Add lids and bands to finger tight.
9. Carefully place jars on rack in canner. Attach and secure canner lid. Heat until canner starts hissing. Allow the steam to escape the vent for 5-10 minutes, add gauge and begin timing after the first jiggle. Process pints for 75 minutes and quarts for 90 minutes at 10 pounds pressure adjusting for altitude.

10. Remove canner from heat. Allow pressure to decrease naturally.
11. Remove lid. Remove jars from the canner after 5 minutes. Cool on a wire rack or kitchen towel. Remove bands, label jars, and store them in a cool, dark place.

# Ground Meat

Convenient to have on hand for soups, stews, sloppy joes, and casseroles since the meat is already cooked and requires no refrigeration.

## INGREDIENTS

- 8 lbs ground beef, lamb, pork, chicken, or turkey
- 5 tsp canning salt
- 2 tsp freshly ground black pepper
- 2 medium onions chopped
- 4 garlic cloves chopped finely
- 3 cups beef broth or stock

## YIELD

14 pints or 7 quarts

## RECIPE

1. Prepare jars, lids, and pressure canner.
2. In a large bowl, combine ground meat, salt, and pepper using your clean hands.
3. Working in batches, brown meat stirring often. Drain fat and set meat aside.
4. Sauté onions and garlic until soft. Mix with browned meat.
5. Heat broth or stock to boiling over medium-high heat, then reduce heat to low.
6. Using a jar funnel, pack the hot meat loosely into the jars, leaving 1-inch headspace.
7. Add hot broth or stock to each jar, leaving 1-inch headspace.
8. Using a rubber spatula, remove air bubbles. Add more liquid if necessary, leaving 1-inch headspace.
9. Wipe rims with a paper towel moistened with vinegar. Add lids and bands to finger tight.
10. Carefully place jars on rack in canner. Attach and secure canner lid. Heat until canner starts hissing. Allow the steam to escape the vent for 5-10 minutes, add gauge and begin timing after the first jiggle. Process pints for 75 minutes and quarts for 90 minutes at 10 pounds pressure. Adjust timing for higher altitudes.

11. Remove canner from heat. Allow pressure to decrease naturally.
12. Remove lid. Remove jars from the canner after 5 minutes. Cool on a wire rack or kitchen towel. Remove bands, label jars, and store them in a cool, dark place.

# Venison and Game

If you're a hunter or prepper, this recipe is right up your alley! Make sure to use high-quality, fresh meat for the best results.

## INGREDIENTS

- Boneless venison or other game
- Canning salt
- Hot broth or stock
- ClearJel (optional)

## YIELD

Varies

## Luke's Variations

You can substitute roast beef, lamb, pork, or veal for game meat. Follow all other instructions. Trim fat after roasting and before canning.

## RECIPE

1. Prepare jars, lids, and pressure canner.
2. Cut meat into ½ to 1-inch strips long enough to fit into the size jar you are using. Roast at 400 degrees in a preheated oven in a large roasting pan until browned on the outside but still pink on the inside. Remove from oven and set aside.
3. Prepare stock by pouring fat from the roasted meat into a measuring cup. For each tablespoon of fat, add 1 cup of boiling water back to the roasting pan. Bring to boil over medium-high heat, scraping up any meat bits stuck to the pan. Add ClearJel, if desired, to thicken the broth. You can also use premade stock or broth in a pinch.
4. Pack hot meat into hot jars, leaving 1-inch headspace. Add ½ teaspoon canning salt to each pint jar or 1 teaspoon to each quart jar. Using a jar funnel, ladle hot broth over meat to cover, leaving 1-inch headspace.
5. Using a rubber spatula, remove air bubbles. Add more broth if necessary, leaving 1-inch headspace.
6. Wipe rims with a paper towel moistened with vinegar. Add lids and bands to finger tight.
7. Carefully place jars on rack in canner. Attach and secure canner lid. Heat until

canner starts hissing. Allow the steam to escape the vent for 5-10 minutes, add gauge and begin timing after the first jiggle. Process pints for 75 minutes and quarts for 90 minutes at 10 pounds pressure. Adjust timing for higher altitudes.

8. Remove canner from heat. Allow pressure to decrease naturally.
9. Remove lid. Remove jars from the canner after 5 minutes. Cool on a wire rack or kitchen towel. Remove bands, label jars, and store them in a cool, dark place.

# Fish

Most people would never think of canning their fresh catch of the day, but you're able to successfully can all fish. Follow the recipe which follows for tuna. Process only in 8oz or pint jars.

## INGREDIENTS

- Fresh fish, bones removed if fish is large
- 1 cup canning salt
- 16 cups water

## YIELD

Varies

## TUNA

The difference when canning tuna is that you don't need to brine the fish before canning. Simply cut the tuna into pieces that will fit in the jars and pack raw. Add ½ teaspoon canning salt per 8oz jar or 1 teaspoon per pint jar. Process both 8oz and pint jars for 100 minutes at 10 pounds pressure. Adjust timing for higher altitudes.

## RECIPE

1. Dissolve canning salt in the water to make a salt-water brine in a large bowl or stainless-steel pot. Remove bones and cut fish into pieces that will fit in the jars. Place fish pieces in the brine and soak in the refrigerator for 1 hour. After time has elapsed, drain in a colander for 15 minutes.
2. Prepare jars, lids, and pressure canner.
3. Pack fish in room-temperature jars with the skin facing out, leaving 1-inch headspace. Do not add any liquid.
4. Wipe rims with a paper towel moistened with vinegar. Add lids and bands to finger tight.
5. Carefully place jars on rack in canner. Attach and secure canner lid. Heat until canner starts hissing. Allow the steam to escape vent for 5-10 minutes, add gauge and begin timing after the first jiggle. Process both 8oz and pint jars for 100 minutes at 10 pounds pressure. Adjust timing for higher altitudes.
6. Remove canner from heat. Allow pressure to decrease naturally.
7. Remove lid. Remove jars from the canner after 5 minutes. Cool on a wire rack or kitchen towel. Remove bands, label jars, and store them in a cool, dark place.

# OTHER PRESERVATION METHODS

In addition to canning, there are many other popular ways to preserve your harvest, so it lasts all year. What follows is a brief overview.

**Freezing**

Modern refrigeration began in the early 20th century. Refrigeration helps to preserve food by storing it at low temperatures to slow down the spread of bacteria and decomposition. When separate freezer units were developed, it took refrigeration one step further by freezing water present in meats, fruits, and vegetables into ice crystals, making it unavailable for bacterial microorganisms that need liquid moisture and air to spread. Separate freezer units became popular after WWII.

Many people swear by freezing their harvest for ease and convenience. With rare exceptions, I don't freeze my harvest for several reasons.

1. Frozen food is dependent on a consistent source of electricity or a generator. If you lose your power for a significant period, you'll have to consume 20 gallons of marinara sauce, or else it will go to waste. Canned food is energy independent and can be stored for 18 months or longer, and I've stored some canned items for as long as 4 years. Canned and dehydrated food is the sustainable prepper choice.

2. You can't transport frozen food easily. Suppose there's an impending flood or crisis, and you must leave home in a hurry. Does it make sense to grab an ice chest full of frozen food or a cardboard box packed with canned soups, stews, and meats? In an emergency, you can eat canned food right out of the jar without reheating. The empty jars can also serve a multitude of purposes if you must bug out.
3. You can't mail frozen food to a loved one. Canned goods make thoughtful and appreciated gifts. And can be used to barter.
4. You would need a huge walk-in freezer to store what you can in a pantry, closet, or cupboard.

## Drying

Drying, or dehydrating, is the oldest method of preserving food, dating back to prehistoric times, and it's still used today. Once most of the water content is removed, dehydrated foods are lightweight and take up little space, making them easily portable. Dehydrated foods are ideal for hikers, campers, and in an emergency. Add water to rehydrate or eat as is. You can make meat jerky, kale chips, banana chips, sun-dried tomatoes, etc.

## Sun & Air

Leaving food in the sun and air causes evaporation of the water content, and this helps prevent bacterial growth as up to 80% of the moisture is removed. This method is free, and it's a traditional and still a popular way to dry herbs, peppers, and tomatoes.

## Oven & Electric

You can use an oven on low heat or an electric dehydrator to dehydrate many foods. You need to be careful not to cook the food. Instead, the goal is to remove as much moisture content as possible.

## Cold Storage

Back in the day, every farm had a root cellar or underground pantry where produce, especially root crops and fruits, would be stored to extend their usable life. In ancient times, people would bury food in ice or underground during the winter months. Many modern-day preppers employ this technique today. As a child, my family always stored root crops, like potatoes, in our unheated cellar where it was colder.

## Salt Curing

When early explorers embarked on voyages that would put them at sea for months, they would pack salt-cured meats and fish in barrels. The meats and fish would be packed in layers with dry salt. The salt drew out moisture, inhibiting the growth of bacteria and slowing the decomposition rate, meaning that certain foodstuffs could last for years if preserved properly. You can also employ salt curing to preserve many herbs. Simply layer the fresh herbs between layers of canning salt in a Mason jar with a lid.

## Fermentation

This is another old way of preserving food that is gaining in popularity today. Fermentation is a natural process through which microorganisms like yeast and bacteria convert carbohydrates into alcohol or acids. The alcohol or acids act as a natural preservative and give fermented foods a distinct zest and tartness. It also promotes the growth of beneficial bacteria known as probiotics. Probiotics have been shown to improve immune function as well as digestive and heart health. Pickles and other vegetables can easily be fermented in a specially-designed crock which allows the gases, created during the fermentation process, to escape.

# TROUBLESHOOTING

Even experienced home canners still have challenges. Here are some troubleshooting tips for a successful output.

**My jars did not seal.**

If your jars did not seal properly, there might have been residue left on the rims before you applied the lids. Or you may have overfilled the jars. Refrigerate these jars and consume them promptly.

**My pickles are soft or mushy.**

So many possibilities. Make sure to slice off the blossom end when preparing cucumbers for pickling. The use of table salt can be an issue so always use canning salt. An improper ratio of vinegar and water could be the culprit. Maybe you used over-ripe cucumbers. Perhaps you packed the cucumbers too tightly in the jar. Maybe your cucumbers were refrigerated for too long. You should always use fresh pickling cucumbers. Soaking cucumbers in ice water, sometimes with salt, will help produce crisper pickles. As found in Ball Pickle Crisp or Xtra Crunch by Mrs. Wages, the use of calcium chloride will help a great deal. You can find these products wherever canning supplies are sold.

## My jars leaked and lost liquid during processing.

You may have packed the food too tightly. The bands may have been too loose, or you did not remove air bubbles before applying the lids.

My jelly or jam didn't set correctly and is runny.

If you attempt to double the recipe, it won't set properly. Make 1 batch at a time. Sometimes it may take up to 2 weeks to set correctly. After 2 weeks, you can remake runny jam or jelly by recooking it and reprocessing it following instructions included with the pectin.

## My jelly or jam has cloudy globs.

The foam, formed by the air content of the fruit, is minuscule air bubbles. Unless it is skimmed off the surface immediately after removing the jam or jelly from the heat, it will create cloudy globs in your product affecting the appearance. The use of a small amount of butter when cooking the jam or jelly will help reduce foaming. Or use margarine if you're vegan. Simply skim the foam off the surface with a large spoon before ladling the product into the jars.

## I didn't get enough juice from the drip bag.

Simply pour sufficient boiling water over the pulp in the drip bag until you accumulate the amount of juice you require. Do not squeeze the bag.

## My salsa is runny.

Your tomatoes probably contained a lot of water. Try not to harvest tomatoes immediately after watering or after a rainfall. You can also squeeze the tomatoes after peeling to remove excess moisture and seeds. You can also cook your salsa longer, uncovered, so that additional liquid evaporates until you reach your desired consistency.

**My soup or stew is too thick.**

Simply add some water when reheating. Or, if you desire a creamy consistency, add some milk or cream when reheating.

**I went to open a stored jar, and the lid lifted right off.**

Your jar did not seal properly. You may have overfilled the jar. There may have been residue left on the rim of the jar before you applied the lid. There may have been the formation of yeast in the canned product because of improper processing. The food is spoiled and must be immediately discarded. Sterilize the jar and band and safely discard the lid.

# CONCLUSION

"Keep calm and can on." Luke Potter

We've come to the end of our home canning journey together, at least for now. We've had fun learning about the history and science of home canning. I hope you can see how easy, economical, and practical home canning can be while enjoying delicious, canned goods with your family and friends. I've included many tips and tricks I've learned over the years that can help you avoid some of the mistakes that are easy to make when you start canning.

As you preserve your own food, you'll find yourself going back to certain recipes repeatedly. Some pages will be earmarked for easy reference. Other pages will be stained with jam. You might make notes in the book or add your own heirloom family recipes in the back. Grandma's recipe cards might be used as bookmarks. Every gardening season means more home canning, and I know you'll come to look forward to those moments you spend in your kitchen just like me. For me and many others, home canning isn't just about the output - it's also about the mental well-being that canning provides. Growing your own food, and then preserving it in the kitchen, seems to chase away clouds of doubt and depression. There are few experiences so simple in life as gardening and home canning that provide you with the self-esteem and confidence that you'll discover by growing and preserving your own food.

Even if you don't have a garden, you can fill your pantry with locally grown fruits and vegetables. Visit your local farmer's market or pick-your-own farms. Stock up on meat when it's on sale and can it. Graciously accept those unwanted zucchinis from your neighbor and make pickles – and then give them a jar. As you've learned in this book, almost anything and everything can be canned successfully when you follow simple instructions. If you can read, you can can.

I could have delved deeper into other food preservation methods, but I'll save those for future books. And if you've struggled with growing your own food in the past, or if you have limited space or experience, refer to Part One of this book, How to Grow Vegetables in Pots & Containers. It's also available as an eBook, paperback, hard cover, and audiobook on Amazon.

I really hope you and your family get to have as much fun as mine when canning season arrives. It's great to get the kids involved so they can learn and pass on these valuable, sustainable life skills. I sincerely hope you take the opportunity to fill your pantry and cupboards with healthy, nutritious home canned food.

The final thought I would like to leave you with before we bid farewell is this - even the smallest pantry is an opportunity for greatness. Treat every situation in life as a new experience. Give it the attention it deserves. Keep an eye on it so it doesn't boil over and wait for the ping! No matter what insurmountable task you are facing, with a bit of love, a little patience, and a little time, you can succeed in anything you do.

I want to give a big thank you to all of you who read this book. I hope you find the content enlightening and that you are motivated to get your pantry and cupboards stocked. There is nothing more satisfying than when you look at what you have accomplished and realize that your family will never go hungry – regardless of what may happen in the future.

If you enjoyed reading this book, please share it with your friends. Consider gifting a copy to a loved one who gardens. And please leave a review on Amazon so that other home canners, preppers, and homesteaders can find the inspiration to preserve their own food. I hope to see you in the canning goods section at the hardware store. I promise, I'll let you take the last box of Mason jars!

Remember, life is abundant!

# ABOUT THE AUTHOR

Luke Potter, The Urban Farmer, is a gardener, homeschool teacher, avid home canner and author of gardening and home canning books. He loves to share gardening and canning advice with both expert and first-timers. His goal is to build a sustainable community of like-minded individuals dedicated to feeding their families healthy, organic food while preserving the traditions of our ancestors. Gardeners as close as your neighbor and as far away as Uganda are sharing his lessons with others. He hopes to assist you on your personal journey while attaining the Zen of a more self-reliant lifestyle. His mantra, "Life is abundant," can be applied to all aspects of your life. Join Luke and his growing grassroots movement. He encourages you to learn to reap what you sow while you help make the world a better place for today and tomorrow.

You can contact Luke on Facebook or by email @
luketheurbanfarmer@aol.com
https://luketheurbanfarmer.com

# RESOURCES

*Canning food processing.* (n.d.). Https://Www.Britannica.Com/Topic/Canning-Food-Processing. https://www.britannica.com/topic/canning-food-processing

*From salt to cold storage rooms: How we've been preserving food over the years.* (2020, May 25). Https://Pindercooling.Com/from-Salt-to-Cold-Storage-Rooms-How-Weve-Been-Preserving-Food-over-the-Years/. https://pindercooling.com/from-salt-to-cold-storage-rooms-how-weve-been-preserving-food-over-the-years/

*How did we can?* (n.d.). Https://Www.Nal.Usda.Gov/Exhibits/Ipd/Canning/Timeline-Table. https://www.nal.usda.gov/exhibits/ipd/canning/timeline-table

Koehler. (2021, July 21). *It's time to can tuna.* Https://Extension.Wsu.Edu/Graysharbor/2021/07/Time-to-Can-Tuna. https://extension.wsu.edu/graysharbor/2021/07/time-to-can-tuna

Pruitt. (2015, May 21). *The juicy 400-year history of pickles.* Https://Www.History.Com/News/Pickles-History-Timeline. https://www.history.com/news/pickles-history-timeline

*Skimming foam from jam: Everything you need to know.* (2017, June 21). Http://Nwedible.Com/Skimming-Jam-Foam-Questions. http://nwedible.com/skimming-jam-foam-questions

*Troubleshooting common problems with home canned pickles.* (n.d.). Https://Extension.Umn.Edu/Preserving-and-Preparing/Pickle-Problems. https://extension.umn.edu/preserving-and-preparing/pickle-problems

Victory Garden. (n.d.). Https://En.Wikipedia.Org/Wiki/Victory_garden. https://en.wikipedia.org/wiki/Victory_garden

*What is my elevation?* (n.d.). Https://Whatismyelevation.Com. https://whatismyelevation.com

*Stay Connected! Facebook discussion group link*
*https://www.facebook.com/groups/501585191212408*

# INDEX OF RECIPES

## A

Apple Butter 111
Apple Cider Butter 110
Apple Jelly 94
Apple Juice 52
Apple Pie Filling 67
Applesauce 57

## B

Banana Pepper Jelly 101
Beef Stew with Vegetables 34
Beets 87
Blueberries 61
Blueberry and Basil Vinegar 157
Blueberry Jam 106
Blueberry Jelly 98
Blueberry Pie Filling 70
Bread and Butter Pickles 122

## C

Canned Chicken 159
Carrot and Orange Marmalade 114
Carrots 85
Chicken a la King 162
Chicken Bone-in 159
Chicken Soup 31
Chili con Carne 42
Cinnamon Apples 64
Clam Chowder 33
Concord Grape Jelly 92
Concord Grape Juice 49
Corn 81
Corn Relish 150
Crabapple Jelly 95
Cranberry Juice 47
Cranberry Sauce 56
Creamed Corn 82
Cucumber and Onion Pickles 120

## D

Dill Pickles 118
Dill Relish 148
Dilly Beans 129
Dilly Carrots 131
Do Chua 132

## F

Fish 168
Fruit Cocktail 54
FRUITS 53
4 Thieves Vinegar Tonic 153

## G

Grapefruit Juice 51
Green Beans 77
Greens 86
Green Tomato Mincemeat 72
Green Tomato Relish 151
Ground Meat 164

## H

Herb Jelly 103
Hungarian Pepper Jelly 102

## I

Ice Water Pickle Spears 126
Italian Bread Soup 38

Italian Meatballs  161

## J

JELLIES, JAMS, FRUIT BUTTERS & MARMALADES  91
JUICES  46

## L

Leek and Potato Soup  40
Lemon and Lavender Jelly  104

## M

Meatless Chili  43
Meatless Mincemeat Pie Filling  71
Meatless Spaghetti Sauce  41
MEAT, POULTRY & FISH  158

## N

New England Boiled Dinner  44

## O

Okra  88
Orange Marmalade  112

## P

Peaches  59
Peach Pie Filling  73
Pears  62
Peas  83
Pickled Hot Pepper Mix  139
Pickled Hot Peppers  141
Pickled Red Cabbage  128
Pickled Three-Bean Salad  137
Pickled Vegetable Mix  127
PICKLES & PICKLED VEGETABLES  117
PIE FILLINGS  66
Pineapple Juice  50
Potatoes  90
Pumpkin or Squash Pie Filling  74

## Q

Queen's Jam  109

## R

Raspberry Jam  108
Raspberry Vinegar  155
Red Cinnamon Apples  64
Red Pepper Relish  149
RELISHES & SALSA  144
Rose Hip Jelly  96

## S

Sauerkraut  136
SOUPS & STEWS  30
Soup Stock  32
Sour Pickles  125
Split Pea Soup  36
Sriracha Pepper Jelly  101
Stewed Tomatoes  79, 80
Strawberry Jam  105
Strawberry Jelly  100
Strawberry Lemon Marmalade  116
Strawberry Rhubarb Pie Filling  69
Sweet Pickled Beets  134
Sweet Pickles  142
Sweet Potatoes  89
Sweet Relish  147

## T

Tarragon Vinegar  156
Taste of Summer Vegetable Salsa  145
Tomato Soup  37
Triple Berry Jam  107
Tuna  168

## V

Vegetable Juice Cocktail  48
VEGETABLES  76
Vegetable Soup  45
Venison and Game  166
VINEGARS  152

## W

Watermelon Rind Pickles  123
Winter Squash  84

# My Canning Journal

Printed in Great Britain
by Amazon